DROPPING
ASHES
ON
THE
BUDDHA

Zen Master Seung Sahn

The
Teaching
of Zen
Master
SEUNG SAHN

Dropping
Ashes
on
the
Buddha

Compiled
and
Edited
by
STEPHEN MITCHELL

Grove Press   **New York**

Published simultaneously in Canada
Printed in the United States of America

Library of Congress Catalog Card Number 75-37236
ISBN 0-8021-3052-6

Designed by Steven A. Baron

Grove Press
841 Broadway
New York, NY 10003

The Providence Zen Center, Inc.
528 Pound Road
Cumberland, RI 02864

03 04 05 06 07 20 19 18 17 16 15 14

Table of Contents

Preface

Zen teaching is like a window. At first, we look *at* it, and see only the dim reflection of our own face. But as we learn, and our vision becomes clear, the teaching becomes clear. Until at last it is perfectly transparent. We see through it. We see all things: our own face.

This book is a collection of Seung Sahn Soen-sa's* teaching in America—dialogues, stories, formal Zen interviews, Dharma Speeches, and letters. The words arise as situations arise. Each situation is a game, and a matter of life and death.

The title comes from a problem which Soen-sa gives his students for homework. It goes like this:

Somebody comes into the Zen Center with a lighted cigarette, walks up to the Buddha-statue, blows smoke in its face and drops ashes on its lap. You are standing there. What can you do?

This person has understood that nothing is holy or unholy. All things in the universe are one, and that one is himself. So everything is permitted. Ashes are Buddha; Buddha is ashes. The cigarette flicks. The ashes drop.

But his understanding is only partial. He has not yet understood that all things are just as they are. Holy is holy; unholy is unholy. Ashes are ashes; Buddha is Buddha. He is very attached to emptiness and to his own understanding, and he thinks that all words are useless. So whatever you say

*Zen Master Seung Sahn is properly written about as *Soen-sa* ("Zen Master"; equivalent to *Zenji* in Japanese) and addressed or spoken about as *Soen-sa-nim* (*nim* being the honorific particle in Korean). *Soen* is pronounced somewhat like "sun," but further back in the throat; *sa* rhymes with "ha"; *nim* sounds like "neem." In his name, the vowel in "Seung" is like the vowel in "look."

to him, however you try to teach him, he will hit you. If you try to teach by hitting him back, he will hit you even harder. (He is very strong.)

How can you cure his delusion?

Since you are a Zen student, you are also a Zen teacher. You are walking on the path of the Bodhisattva, whose vow is to save all beings from their suffering. This person is suffering from a mistaken view. You must help him understand the truth: that all things in the universe are just as they are.

How can you do this?

If you find the answer to this problem, you will find the true way.

Introduction

Deep in the mountains, the great temple bell is struck. You hear it reverberating in the morning air, and all thoughts disappear from your mind. There is nothing that is you; there is nothing that is not you. There is only the sound of the bell, filling the whole universe.

Springtime comes. You see the flowers blossoming, the butterflies flitting about; you hear the birds singing, you breathe in the warm weather. And your mind is only springtime. It is nothing at all.

You visit Niagara and take a boat to the bottom of the Falls. The downpouring of the water is in front of you and around you and inside you, and suddenly you are shouting: YAAAAAA!

In all these experiences, outside and inside have become one. This is Zen mind.

Original nature has no opposites. Speech and words are not necessary. Without thinking, all things are exactly as they are. The truth is just like this.

Then why do we use words? Why have we made this book?

According to Oriental medicine, when you have a hot sickness you should take hot medicine. Most people are very attached to words and speech. So we cure this sickness with word-and-speech medicine.

Most people have a deluded view of the world. They don't see it as it is; they don't understand the truth. What is good, what is bad? Who makes good, who makes bad? They cling to their opinions with all their might. But everybody's opinion is different. How can you say that your opinion is correct and somebody else's is wrong? This is delusion.

If you want to understand the truth, you must let go of your situation, your condition, and all your opinions. Then your mind will be before thinking. "Before thinking" is clear mind. Clear mind has no inside and no outside. It is just like this. "Just like this" is the truth.

An eminent teacher said,

> If you want to pass through this gate,
> do not give rise to thinking.

This means that if you are thinking, you can't understand Zen. If you keep the mind that is before thinking, this is Zen mind.

So another Zen Master said,

> Everything the Buddha taught
> was only to correct your thinking.
> If already you have cut off thinking,
> what good are the Buddha's words?

The Heart Sutra says, "Form is emptiness, emptiness is form." This means, "no form, no emptiness." But the true meaning of "no form, no emptiness" is, "form is form, emptiness is emptiness."

If you are thinking, you won't understand these words. If you are not thinking, "just like this" is Buddha-nature.

What is Buddha-nature?

Deep in the mountains, the great temple bell is struck. The truth is just like this.

Seung Sahn

DROPPING
ASHES
ON
THE
BUDDHA

1. Zen Is Understanding Yourself

One day a student from Chicago came to the Providence Zen Center and asked Seung Sahn Soen-sa, "What is Zen?"

Soen-sa held his Zen stick above his head and said, "Do you understand?"

The student said, "I don't know."

Soen-sa said, "This don't-know mind is you. Zen is understanding yourself."

"What do you understand about me? Teach me."

Soen-sa said, "In a cookie factory, different cookies are baked in the shape of animals, cars, people, and airplanes. They all have different names and forms, but they are all made from the same dough, and they all taste the same.

"In the same way, all things in the universe—the sun, the moon, the stars, mountains, rivers, people, and so forth—have different names and forms, but they are all made from the same substance. The universe is organized into pairs of opposites: light and darkness, man and woman, sound and silence, good and bad. But all these opposites are mutual, because they are made from the same substance. Their names and their forms are different, but their substance is the same. Names and forms are made by your thinking. If you are not thinking and have no attachment to name and form, then all substance is one. Your don't-know mind cuts off all thinking. This is your substance. The substance of this Zen stick and your own substance are the same. You are this stick; this stick is you."

The student said, "Some philosophers say this substance is energy, or mind, or God, or matter. Which is the truth?"

Soen-sa said, "Four blind men went to the zoo and visited the elephant. One blind man touched its side and said, 'The elephant is like a wall.' The next blind man touched its trunk and said, 'The elephant is like a snake.' The next blind man touched its leg and said, 'The elephant is like a column.' The last blind man touched its tail and said, 'The elephant is like a broom.' Then the four blind men started to fight, each one believing that his opinion was the right one. Each only understood the part he had touched; none of them understood the whole.

"Substance has no name and no form. Energy, mind, God, and matter are all name and form. Substance is the Absolute. Having name and form is having opposites. So the whole world is like the blind men fighting among themselves. Not understanding yourself is not understanding the truth. That is why there is fighting among ourselves. If all the people in the world understood themselves, they would attain the Absolute. Then the world would be at peace. World peace is Zen."

The student said, "How can practicing Zen make world peace?"

Soen-sa said, "People desire money, fame, sex, food, and rest. All this desire is thinking. Thinking is suffering. Suffering means no world peace. Not thinking is not suffering. Not suffering means world peace. World peace is the Absolute. The Absolute is I."

The student said, "How can I understand the Absolute?"

Soen-sa said, "You must understand yourself."

"How can I understand myself?"

Soen-sa held up the Zen stick and said, "Do you see this?"

He then quickly hit the table with the stick and said, "Do you hear this? This stick, this sound, and your mind—are they the same or different?

The student said, "The same."

Soen-sa said, "If you say they are the same, I will hit you thirty times. If you say they are different, I will still hit you thirty times. Why?"

The student was silent.

Soen-sa shouted "KATZ!!!"* Then he said, "Spring comes, the grass grows by itself."

---

*This is the famous Zen belly-shout. Its transcription (KATZ in Korean and Japanese, HO in Chinese) hardly does it justice.

2. The Zen Circle

One evening, at the Providence Zen Center, Seung Sahn Soen-sa gave the following Dharma Speech:

"What is Zen? Zen is understanding myself. What am I?

"I explain Zen by means of a circle. There are five points marked on the circle: zero degrees, ninety degrees, one-hundred-eighty degrees, two-hundred-seventy degrees, and three-hundred-sixty degrees. 360° is exactly the same point as 0°.

"We begin from 0° to 90°. This is the area of thinking and attachment. Thinking is desire, desire is suffering. All things are separated into opposites: good and bad, beautiful and ugly, mine and yours. I like this; I don't like that. I try to get happiness and avoid suffering. So life here is suffering, and suffering is life.

"Past 90° is the area of the Consciousness or Karma I. Below 90° there is attachment to name and form. Here there is attachment to thinking. Before you were born, you were zero; now you are one; in the future, you will die and again become zero. So zero equals one, one equals zero. All things here are the same, because they are of the same substance. All things have name and form, but their names and forms come from emptiness and will return to emptiness. This is still thinking.

"At 180° there is no thinking at all. This is the experience of true emptiness. Before thinking, there are no words and

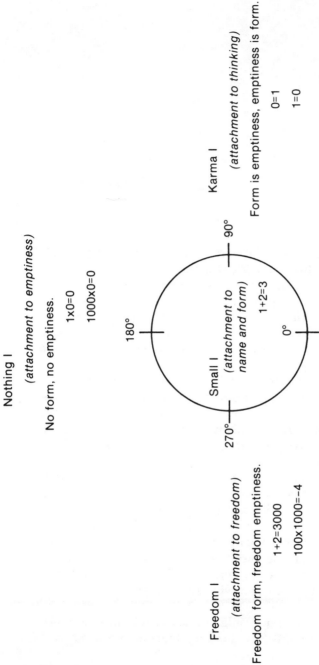

Nothing I

(attachment to emptiness)

No form, no emptiness.

$$1 \times 0 = 0$$
$$1000 \times 0 = 0$$

Karma I

(attachment to thinking)

Form is emptiness, emptiness is form.

$$0 = 1$$
$$1 = 0$$

Small I

(attachment to name and form)

$$1 + 2 = 3$$

Big I

(no-attachment thinking)

Form is form, emptiness is emptiness.

$$3 \times 3 = 9$$

Freedom I

(attachment to freedom)

Freedom form, freedom emptiness.

$$1 + 2 = 3000$$
$$100 \times 1000 = -4$$

90°

180°

0°

360°

270°

no speech. So there are no mountains, no rivers, no God, no Buddha, nothing at all. There is only . . ." At this point Soen-sa hit the table.

"Next is the area up to 270°, the area of magic and miracles. Here, there is complete freedom, with no hindrance in space or time. This is called live thinking. I can change my body into a snake's. I can ride a cloud to the Western Heaven. I can walk on water. If I want life, I have life; if I want death, I have death. In this area, a statue can cry; the ground is not dark or light; the tree has no roots; the valley has no echo.

"If you stay at 180°, you become attached to emptiness. If you stay at 270°, you become attached to freedom.

"At 360°, all things are just as they are; the truth is just like this. 'Like this' means that there is no attachment to anything. This point is exactly the same as the zero point: we arrive where we began, where we have always been. The difference is that 0° is attachment thinking, while 360° is no-attachment thinking.

"For example, if you drive a car with attachment thinking, your mind will be somewhere else and you will go through the red light. No-attachment thinking means that your mind is clear all the time. When you drive, you aren't thinking; you are just driving. So the truth is just like this. Red light means Stop; green light means Go. It is intuitive action. Intuitive action means acting without any desire or attachment. My mind is like a clear mirror, reflecting everything just as it is. Red comes, and the mirror becomes red; yellow comes, and the mirror becomes yellow. This is how a Bodhisattva lives. I have no desires for myself. My actions are for all people.

"0° is Small I. 90° is Karma I. 180° is Nothing I. 270° is Freedom I. 360° is Big I. Big I is infinite time, infinite space. So there is no life and no death. I only wish to save all people. If people are happy, I am happy; if people are sad, I am sad.

"Zen is reaching 360°. When you reach 360°, all degrees on the circle disappear. The circle is just a Zen teaching-device. It doesn't really exist. We use it to simplify thinking and to test a student's understanding."

Soen-sa then held up a book and a pencil and said, "This book and this pencil—are they the same or different? At 0°, they are different. At 90°, since all things are one, the book is the pencil, the pencil is the book. At 180°, all thinking is cut off, so there are no words and no speech. The answer is only . . ." Here Soen-sa hit the table. "At 270°, there is perfect freedom, so a good answer is: the book is angry, the pencil laughs. Finally, at 360°, the truth is just like this. Spring comes, the grass grows by itself. Inside it is light, outside it is dark. Three times three equals nine. Everything is as it is. So the answer here is: the book is the book, the pencil is the pencil.

"So at each point the answer is different. Which one is the correct answer? Do you understand?

"Now here is an answer for you: all five answers are wrong.

"Why?"

After waiting a few moments, Soen-sa shouted "KATZ!!!" and then said, "The book is blue, the pencil is yellow. If you understand this, you will understand yourself.

"But if you understand yourself, I will hit you thirty times. And if you don't understand yourself, I will still hit you thirty times.

"Why?"

After again waiting a few moments, Soen-sa said, "It is very cold today."

3. My Dharma Is Too Expensive

Once a student came to Zen Master Hyang Bong and said, "Master, please teach me the Dharma."

Hyang Bong said, "I'm sorry, but my Dharma is very expensive."

"How much does it cost?"

"How much can you pay?"

The student put his hand into his pocket and took out some coins. "This is all the money I have."

"Even if you offered me a pile of gold as big as a mountain," said Hyang Bong, "my Dharma would still be too expensive."

So the student went off to practice Zen. After a few months of hard training, he returned to Hyang Bong and said, "Master, I will give you my life, I will do anything for you, I will be your slave. Please teach me."

Hyang Bong said, "Even if you offered me a thousand lives, my Dharma would still be too expensive."

Quite dejected, the student went off again. After several more months of hard training, he returned and said, "I will give you my mind. Will you teach me now?"

Hyang Bong said, "Your mind is a pail of stinking garbage. I have no use for it. And even if you offered me ten thousand minds, my Dharma would still be too expensive."

Again the student left to do hard training. After some time he came to an understanding that the whole universe is empty. So he returned to the Master and said, "Now I understand how expensive your Dharma is."

Hyang Bong said, "How expensive is it?"

The student shouted "KATZ!!!"

Hyang Bong said, "No, it's more expensive than that."

This time, when he left, the student was thoroughly confused and in deep despair. He vowed not to see the Master again until he had attained the supreme awakening. Eventually that day came, and he returned. "Master, now I truly understand: the sky is blue, the grass is green."

"No no no," said Hyang Bong. "My Dharma is even more expensive than that."

At this, the student grew furious. "I already understand, I don't need your Dharma, you can take it and shove it up your ass!"

Hyang Bong laughed. That made the student even angrier. He wheeled around and stomped out of the room. Just as he was going out the door, Hyang Bong called to him, "Wait a minute!"

The student turned his head.

"Don't lose my Dharma," said Hyang Bong.

Upon hearing these words, the student was enlightened.

4. Advice to a Beginner

February 16, 1975

Dear Soen-sa-nim,

Wednesday evening I attended a discussion you presented at Yale with the assistance of two students. I was keenly interested in merely seeing you and in hearing your words and in seeing other interested people, because my interest in Zen has so far developed solely through my own efforts, and my knowledge of it has come only through books. And this approach has made Zen seem remote and inapplicable to this time and life. This has, in turn, generated some feelings that my interest in Zen is an unhealthy attempt to escape this world that I do not understand. Seeing other live people, functioning with ease in this world, relieves some of those feelings and encourages my interest in Zen. This direct experience with Zen also releases a flood of questions about Zen practice. And, finally, we arrive at the point of this letter.

Can you recommend a specific method of *zazen* for a beginner? I have been practicing about one month, sitting, counting exhalations to ten. Do you recommend I continue this method or change? Also, can you give advice on the way to function day-to-day prior to a final understanding? I try doing what has to be done without discursive thinking, with some success; but I have not dispelled a conviction that there is or should be a more concrete guideline for action. I think, particularly, about certain precepts I've read, sixteen in all. Are these precepts just for those who have attained understanding—ways of acting that come only from that understanding? Or can they be applied externally to one without the final understanding, serving as a reference point for actions along the way to attaining understanding?

I have also read of an event termed *sesshin* in which lay people spend a week or so at a temple or center to practice and speak with a Master. Do your centers have such events? If so, please forward specific details.

I am also encountering some confusion in the relation of actual practice to the verbal history of Zen, verbal examples and explanations of the final understanding, etc. I have read histories, examples, and explanations enough to feel I agree intellectually and can comprehend with my reason. But I do not understand in my bones, because there has been no direct experience. So, I agree with those who say that we can't reach understanding through words; it must come through practice. But you use words to help students understand. And I don't understand. In reading, I have thought and thought and always come to that brick wall beyond which words cannot go. So I've pretty much stopped trying to reason out what the words may indicate and try only to practice, sitting *zazen* and thinking about who or what writes these words, eats, sleeps, etc. But I wonder if I am giving up on words without truly exhausting them? I fear this is a confused accounting of confused thoughts, but perhaps you can see through all my delusions.

I have taken enough of your time and greatly appreciate your attention to my questions.

Sincerely,
Patricia

February 23, 1975

Dear Patricia,

Thank you for your letter. How are you?

In your letter, you said that you have read many books about Zen. That's good. But if you are thinking, you can't understand Zen. Anything that can be written in a book, anything that can be said—all this is thinking. If you are thinking, then all Zen books, all Buddhist sutras, all Bibles are demons' words. But if you read with a mind that has cut off all thinking, then Zen books, sutras, and Bibles are all the truth. So is the barking of a dog or the crowing of a rooster: all things are teaching you at every moment, and these sounds are even better teaching than Zen books. So Zen is keeping the mind which is before thinking. Sciences and academic studies are after thinking. We must return to before thinking. Then we will attain our true self.

In your letter you said that your practice has been counting exhalations to ten. This method is not good, not bad. It is possible to practice in this way when you are sitting. But when you are driving, when you are talking, when you are watching television, when you are playing tennis—how is it possible to count your breaths then? Sitting is only a small part of practicing Zen. The true meaning of sitting Zen is to cut off all thinking and to keep not-moving mind. So I ask you: What are you? You don't know; there is only "I don't know." Always keep this don't-know mind. When this don't-know mind becomes clear, then you will understand. So if you keep don't-know mind when you are driving, this is driving Zen. If you keep it when you are talking, this is talking Zen. If you keep it when you are watching television, this is television Zen. You must keep don't-know mind always and everywhere. This is the true practice of Zen.

> The Great Way is not difficult
> if you do not make distinctions.
> Only throw away likes and dislikes,
> and everything will be perfectly clear.

So throw away all opinions, all likes and dislikes, and only keep the mind that doesn't know. This is very important. Don't-know mind is the mind that cuts off all thinking. When all thinking has been cut off, you become empty mind. This is before thinking. Your before-thinking mind, my before-thinking mind, all people's before-thinking minds are the same. This is your substance. Your substance, my substance, and the substance of the whole universe become one. So the tree, the mountain, the cloud, and you become one. Then I ask you: Are the mountain and you the same or different? If you say "the same," I will hit you thirty times. If you say "different," I will still hit you thirty times. Why?

The mind that becomes one with the universe is before thinking. Before thinking there are no words. "Same" and "different" are opposites words; they are from the mind that separates all things. That is why I will hit you if you say either one. So what would be a good answer? If you don't understand, only keep don't-know mind for a while, and you will soon have a good answer. If you do, please send it to me.

You asked why I use words to teach, if understanding through words is impossible. Words are not necessary. But they are very necessary. If you are attached to words, you cannot return to your true self. If you are not attached to words, soon you will attain enlightenment. So if you are thinking, words are very bad. But if you are not thinking, all words and all things that you can see or hear or smell or taste or touch will help you. So it is very important for you to cut off your thinking and your attachment to words.

Here is a poem for you:

> Buddha said all things have Buddha-nature.
> Jo-ju said the dog has no Buddha-nature.
> Which one is correct?
> If you open your mouth, you fall into hell.
> Why?
> KATZ!!!
> Clouds float up to the sky.
> Rain falls down to the ground.

Sincerely yours,
S. S.

P.S. *Sesshin* is the Japanese name for "meditation retreat." In Korean the name is *Yong Maeng Jong Jin,* which means "when sitting, to leap like a tiger." We have one retreat every month at each of our centers: a seven-day retreat in Providence, from the first to the seventh of every month; and three-day retreats in New Haven (beginning the second Friday of the month), in Cambridge (beginning the third Friday), and in New York (beginning the fourth Thursday). You are welcome to come to any of these retreats.

April 6, 1975

Dear Soen-sa-nim,

Thank you for your reply to my last letter. I have been trying to do as you advised, keeping don't-know mind in every activity, but with difficulty. Often, the difficulties involved get me down, for it seems next to impossible to clear out all the rubbish I've accumulated over the years. As my mind returns to the question of whether the mountain and I are the same or different, I often cry and often leave the question. It seems an overwhelming question.

At the beginning, I was very enthusiastic and cheerful and industrious. My enthusiasm wanes and I am not very cheerful or industrious and realizing this makes me even less cheerful. What advice for a failing spirit?

I look forward to the opening of a Zen Center in New Haven. Perhaps the fellowship and opportunity to speak with you and others will revitalize my practice.

Most sincerely,
Patricia

April 11, 1975

Dear Patricia,

Thank you for your letter. You say that keeping don't-know mind is difficult. If you check your thinking mind, then it is difficult. You mustn't check your thinking mind. Thinking is okay; don't worry about it. If you are not upset by your thinking, then it is not difficult to keep don't-know mind. At first you will be able to keep it only for a short time. But if you practice with sincerity, it will keep growing by itself.

Your mind is like the sea. When the wind comes, there are very big waves. When the wind dies down, the waves become smaller and smaller, until finally the wind disappears altogether and the sea is like a clear mirror. Then mountains and trees and all things are reflected on the surface of the sea. There are many thought-waves now in your mind. But if you continue to practice don't-know mind, this thinking will become gradually smaller, until finally your mind will always be clear. When the mind becomes clear, it is like a mirror: red comes and the mirror is red; yellow comes and the mirror is yellow; a mountain comes and the mirror is a mountain. Your mind is the mountain; the mountain is your mind. They are not two. So it is very important not to be attached either to thinking or to not-thinking. You mustn't be upset by anything that goes on in your mind. Only don't worry and keep don't-know mind.

You say that in the beginning you were enthusiastic and now you are discouraged. Both extremes are no good. It is like a guitar string: if you make it too tight, it will be out of tune and will soon snap; if you make it too loose, it will still be out of tune and will not play. You must tune it just right. Too enthusiastic is no good, too discouraged is also no good. Zen mind is everyday mind. You must keep this mind during every action—eating, talking, playing tennis, watching television. Always keep don't-know mind. What is most important is how you keep your mind at this very moment. Just-now mind. If you have free time, it is good to sit. If you don't have free time, then just do action Zen. But be very careful about wanting enlightenment. This is a bad Zen sickness. When you keep a clear mind, the whole universe is you, you are the universe. So you have already attained enlightenment. Wanting enlightenment is only thinking. It is something extra, like painting legs on the picture of a snake. Already the snake is complete as it is. Already the truth is right before your eyes.

Our New Haven Zen Center will be opening soon. It is very true that contact with other Zen students will help your practice. Together-action is very important for Zen students. Bowing together, chanting together, sitting together, eating together—this means that your own situation, your condition, and your opinions can disappear much more easily. Zen work is becoming empty mind. Becoming empty mind means having all your opinions fall away. Then you will experience true emptiness. When you experience true emptiness, you will attain your true situation, your true condition, and your true opinions. I hope that you will come often to the New Haven Zen Center, do hard training, soon attain enlightenment, and save all people from suffering.

Sincerely yours,
S. S.

April 14, 1975

Dear Soen-sa-nim,

Thank you so much for your reply to my letter. It was encouraging and has helped steady my practice and mind.

I am still having some difficulty in practice, however. When I first became keenly interested in Zen, about four months ago, it was after reading some books about Zen. These books served to shatter most remaining structural beliefs for my life and set me adrift. I realized then that I did not understand anything, so everything became a question. Now, in practice, if I ask "Who am I?", I *know* I do not know. It is, therefore, difficult to question in that particular sense with much intensity. I can listen and watch, but it is difficult to question specifically because I have no particular point from which to direct a question. I guess I am worrying about the form of the question, which is irrelevant, and should, instead, just question, in whatever form, with all my being. Is this correct?

There is one more thing I would like to comment upon. Now that I am more fully accepting Zen as a natural function in my life, I feel a strong infusion of love; through your letters, through Mu Gak and other students I have talked with, and in and through myself. I love my family and friends as never before, and this world seems more wonder-

ful than I will ever know. Even if I never attain enlightenment, Zen practice will still have granted me so much for
which to be grateful.

Sincerely yours,
Patricia

May 3, 1975

Dear Patricia,

Thank you for your letter. Please excuse my lateness in
answering, but I was in New York until a few days ago, for
the opening of our Zen Center there, and your letter was not
forwarded. So I didn't receive it until yesterday.

You said that we have helped your practice. This is very
good. Zen practice is of the greatest importance. You must
decide to practice and very strongly keep this decision. This
requires great faith, great courage, and great questioning.

What is great faith? Great faith means that at all times
you keep the mind which decided to practice, no matter
what. It is like a hen sitting on her eggs. She sits on them
constantly, caring for them and giving them warmth, so that
they will hatch. If she becomes careless or negligent, the eggs
will not hatch and become chicks. So Zen mind means always and everywhere believing in myself. I vow to become
Buddha and save all people.

Next—what is great courage? This means bringing all
your energy to one point. It is like a cat hunting a mouse. The
mouse has retreated into its hole, but the cat waits outside
the hole for hours on end without the slightest movement.
It is totally concentrated on the mouse-hole. This is Zen
mind—cutting off all thinking and directing all your energy
to one point.

Next—great questioning. This is like a child who thinks
only of its mother, or a man dying of thirst who thinks only
of water. It is called One Mind. If you question with great
sincerity, there will only be don't-know mind.

If you keep these three—great faith, great courage, and
great questioning—you will soon attain enlightenment. You
said in your letter that practice is difficult. This is thinking.

Zen is not difficult. If you say it is difficult, that means you have been checking yourself, checking your situation, your condition, your opinions. So you say Zen is difficult. But if you keep the mind that is before thinking, then Zen is not difficult. And it is not easy. It is only as it is. Don't make difficult, don't make easy. Just practice.

You said that the Zen books which you read shattered your beliefs. That's very good. But shattered is not shattered. Before, your view was a deluded view. Now it is a correct view. What you believed before was like wanting to hold the rainbow. But the rainbow soon disappears. It never really existed. All things are like this. Before, you believed that all things existed. But now you understand that all things are emptiness. Even so, you must take one step further. Believing or not believing, shattered or not shattered—this is still the area of opposites. You must throw all these opposites away. Then the truth will be only like this. You said that everything was shattered. But this "shattered" is still an attachment to name and form. Originally, there is only emptiness. There is neither shattered nor not shattered. This is the area of the Absolute. The Absolute is true emptiness. True emptiness is before thinking. Before thinking is like this. Form is form, emptiness is emptiness. So your don't-know mind is true emptiness, is before thinking, is the Absolute, is your true self. The names are all different, but they are all names for clear mind. Originally clear mind has no name and no form. There are no words for it. So if you open your mouth, you are wrong. This is why whenever Zen Master Lin-chi was asked a question he only shouted "KATZ!!!" Dok Sahn would answer only by hitting the questioner. Ku-ji would just hold up one finger. If you are not attached to KATZ or HIT or one finger, then you will understand that the meaning behind these actions is only clear mind. The different actions are just different styles of pointing to clear mind. It is impossible to explain clear mind in words, so the Zen Masters used shouting and hitting and holding up one finger to explain. You must put it down! KATZ is only KATZ, HIT is only HIT, one finger is only one finger. You must understand this. When you say, "I know I don't know," this is no good. Don't check your don't-know mind.

Life is Zen. But some people say that life is suffering. How are these different? If you make "my life is Zen," then your life becomes Zen. If somebody else makes "my life is suffering," then that person's life becomes suffering. So it all depends on how you are keeping your mind just now, at this very moment! This just-now mind continues and becomes your life, as one point continues and becomes a straight line. You like Zen, so your life has become Zen. Now you think that the world is wonderful. Your *mind* is wonderful, so the whole world is wonderful. If you attain enlightenment, you will understand that all people are suffering greatly, so your mind also will be suffering. This is big suffering. So you must enter the great Bodhisattva way and save all people from their suffering. I hope that you only keep don't-know mind, always and everywhere. Then you will soon attain enlightenment and save all beings.

Here is a question for you: Somebody once asked the great Zen Master Dong Sahn, "What is Buddha?" Dong Sahn answered, "Three pounds of flax." What does this mean?

I will wait for a good answer.

Sincerely yours,
S. S.

5. Inside, Outside

One Thursday evening, after a Dharma talk at the New Haven Zen Center, a student asked Seung Sahn Soen-sa, "It seems that in Christianity God is outside me, whereas in Zen God is inside me, so God and I are one. Is this correct?"

Soen-sa said, "Where is inside? Where is outside?"

"Inside is in here; outside is out there."

"How can you separate? Where is the boundary line?"

"I'm inside my skin, and the world is outside it."

Soen-sa said, "This is your body's skin. Where is your mind's skin?"

"Mind has no skin."

"Then where is mind?"

"Inside my head."

"Ah, your mind is very small." (Loud laughter from the audience.) "You must keep your mind big. Then you will understand that God, Buddha, and the whole universe fit into your mind." Then, holding up his watch, Soen-sa said, "Is this watch outside your mind or inside it?"

"Outside."

"If you say 'outside,' I will hit you. If you say 'inside,' I will still hit you."

"I don't care—I still say it's outside!"

"If it is outside, how do you know that this is a watch? Does your mind fly out of your eyes and touch the watch and fly back inside?"

"I see the watch. I'm inside, and the watch is outside."

There were a few moments of silence. Soen-sa said, "Don't make inside or outside. Okay?"

The student, still looking doubtful, bowed.

6. A Child Asks About Death

One evening, Katz, a black cat with a white-tipped tail who lived at the Cambridge Zen Center, died after a long illness. The seven-year-old daughter of one of Seung Sahn Soen-sa's students was troubled by the death. After the burial and chanting to Amita Buddha, she went to Soen-sa for an interview.

Soen-sa said, "Do you have any questions?"

Gita said, "Yes. What happened to Katzie? Where did he go?"

Soen-sa said, "Where do you come from?"

"From my mother's belly."

"Where does your mother come from?"

Gita was silent.

Soen-sa said, "Everything is the world comes from the same one thing. It is like in a cookie factory. Many different kinds of cookies are made—lions, tigers, elephants, houses, people. They all have different shapes and different names, but they are all made from the same dough and they all taste the same. So all the different things that you see—a cat, a person, a tree, the sun, this floor—all these things are really the same."

"What are they?"

"People give them many different names. But in themselves, they have no names. When you are thinking, all things have different names and different shapes. But when you are not thinking, all things are the same. There are no words for them. People make the words. A cat doesn't say, 'I am a cat.' People say, 'This is a cat.' The sun doesn't say, 'My name is sun.' People say, 'This is the sun.' So when someone asks you, 'What is this?', how should you answer?"

"I shouldn't use words."

Soen-sa said, "Very good! You shouldn't use words. So if someone asks you, 'What is Buddha?', what would be a good answer?"

Gita was silent.

Soen-sa said, "Now *you* ask *me.*"

"What is Buddha?"

Soen-sa hit the floor.

Gita laughed.

Soen-sa said, "Now *I* ask *you:* What is Buddha?"

Gita hit the floor.

"What is God?"

Gita hit the floor.

"What is your mother?"

Gita hit the floor.

"What are you?"

Gita hit the floor.

"Very good! This is what all things in the world are made of. You and Buddha and God and your mother and the whole world are the same."

Gita smiled.

Soen-sa said, "Do you have any more questions?"

"You still haven't told me where Katz went."

Soen-sa leaned over, looked into her eyes, and said, "You already understand."

Gita said, "Oh!" and hit the floor very hard. Then she laughed.

Soen-sa said, "Very very good! That is how you should answer any question. That is the truth."

Gita bowed and left. As she was opening the door, she turned to Soen-sa and said, "But I'm not going to answer that way when I'm in school. I'm going to give regular answers!"

Soen-sa laughed.

7. Who Needs a Zen Master

One Thursday evening, after a Dharma talk at the Cambridge Zen Center, a student asked Seung Sahn Soen-sa, "Is it necessary to have a Zen Master, and why?"

Soen-sa said, "Why did you come here?"

The student was silent.

Soen-sa said, "If you are thinking, it is necessary. If you

have cut off all thinking, it is not necessary. If your mind is clear, a Zen Master is not necessary, Buddha is not necessary, all things are not necessary."

8. *You* Are Attached!

One evening, after a Dharma talk at Yale University, a student asked Seung Sahn Soen-sa, "What is clear mind?"

Soen-sa held up his watch and said, "What is this?"

The student said, "A watch."

Soen-sa said, "You are attached to name and form. This is not a watch."

"What is it?"

"You already understand."

The student was silent for a moment, then again asked, "What is it?"

Soen-sa said, "You already understand! You can see it, I can see it." (Laughter from the audience.)

The student said, "Thank you."

Soen-sa said, "That's all?" (Laughter.) "What did you understand?"

"I don't know."

Soen-sa pointed to a cup and said, "This is a cup. But the Diamond Sutra says, 'All things that appear in the world are transient. If you view all appearances as non-appearance, then you will see the true nature of everything.' So if you are attached to the form of this cup, you don't understand the truth. If you say this is a cup, you are attached to name and form. But if you say it is not a cup, you are attached to emptiness. Is this a cup or not?"

The student was silent. Then he said, "I'm stuck."

Soen-sa said, "Okay, I will answer for you." He picked up the cup and drank the water in it. "Only this." Then, after a few moments, he said, "All things have names and forms. But who made these names, who made these forms? The sun doesn't say 'My name is sun.' People say, 'This is the sun, this is the moon, this is a mountain, this is a river.' Then who made names and forms? They are made by thinking."

"Who made thinking?"

Soen-sa laughed and said, "Just *you* made thinking!" (Laughter.) "So Zen mind means returning to original mind. Original mind is before thinking. After thinking, there are opposites. Before thinking, there are no opposites. This is the Absolute. There are no words or speech. If you open your mouth, you are wrong. So before thinking is clear mind. In clear mind there is no inside and no outside. What color is that wall? White. This mind. Only white. My mind and this white become one. What is this? This is a watch. Your answer was correct. But when I said, 'You are attached to name and form,' you soon began to think: 'Oh, what was wrong with my answer? What answer can I give that won't be attached to name and form?' This kind of thinking. You were attached to what I said. But I said that only to test your mind. If you weren't attached to my words, you could have said to me, 'You are attached to my words.' This is a good answer. I say to you, 'You are attached to name and form.' Then you say to me, '*You* are attached to my words.'" (Laughter.) "When you asked me, 'What is it?' I answered, 'Already you understand.'" Soen-sa laughed and continued, "This is before thinking.

"So if you cut off all thinking, the universe and you become one. Your substance and the substance of the whole universe are the same. So this cup is you, you are this cup. They are not two. If you are thinking, they are different.

"Now I have explained everything. So I ask you: Are this cup and you the same or different?"

The student said, "You already know."

Soen-sa said, "I don't know. So I am asking you."

"You already understand."

"So I ask *you*!"

"There's clear water in it."

"You are attached to clear water."

"*You* are attached to clear water!" (Laughter.)

Soen-sa laughed and said, "Very good! Now you understand. The cup is filled with clear water. The wall is white. Zen mind is everyday mind. That's all."

9. About the Heart Sutra

November 21, 1974

Dear Soen-sa-nim,

I have some questions concerning the Heart Sutra:

1. The Sutra says that in Nirvana there is "no-attainment, with nothing to attain." But then it says, "All Buddhas of past, present, and future depend on Prajna Paramita and attain Anuttara Samyak Sambodhi." Why is Nirvana not attained, but complete enlightenment, Anuttara Samyak Sambodhi, *is* attained?

2. What is the difference between Nirvana and Anuttara Samyak Sambodhi—between 180° and "like this"—such that 180° is not attained and 360° is attained?

3. When the mind disappears at 180°, doesn't the "like this" mind automatically appear?

4. The first part of the Sutra says, "Form is emptiness, emptiness is form." But the second part says, "In emptiness there is no form." One sentence says they are identical, one

sentence says they are not. I think I understand, but can you say something about this?

Sincerely,
Ed

November 29, 1974

Dear Ed,

Thank you for your letter. How are you doing lately? Is it good or bad?

In answer to your questions:

1. "Why is Nirvana not attained?"—I hit you.
   "Why is Anuttara Samyak Sambodhi attained?"—The sky is blue, the grass is green.

Do you understand my answers? Then you understand no-attainment and attainment.

2. You ask about the difference between Nirvana and Anuttara Samyak Sambodhi. Nirvana is like an empty mirror —no good, no bad, no color, no form, no anything. But when yellow comes, the mirror reflects yellow; when red comes, the mirror becomes red. To dwell in Nirvana for a long time is to be attached to emptiness. This is no good, because then you can't save all people. In Nirvana there are no people, no Buddhas, no suffering, no happiness—only quiet. So it is being attached to this serenity, being attached to your own peace. But past 180°, you arrive at 360°. Then everything is clear. Happiness is happiness; suffering is suffering. So when you meet people who are suffering, you save them from their suffering. When you meet people who are happy, you are happy together. You must teach the true way. The true way is the great Bodhisattva way. If you find the great Bodhisattva way, this is 360°.

3. You ask, "When the mind disappears at 180°, doesn't the 'like this' mind automatically appear?" 180° is only true empty mind. "Like this" mind is the mind that neither appears nor disappears. But what is true empty mind? What is the mind that neither appears nor disappears? It is very necessary not to be attached to name and form. 180° and "like this" are only teaching words. Don't be attached to words.

4. "Form is emptiness, emptiness is form."—This is 90°.
"No form, no emptiness."—This is 180°.

But if you are not attached to words, these two are the same. So we divide: form is emptiness, emptiness is form; no form, no emptiness. Next, *gate gate paragate parasamgate bodhi swaha*. This means that form is form, emptiness is emptiness. You must understand these three kinds. But of these three, which one is correct?

If you say that any are correct, I will hit you thirty times. But if you say that none are correct, I will still hit you thirty times.

So what is the true meaning of the Heart Sutra?

Here is a poem for you:

> After so much suffering in Nirvanic castles,
> what a joy to sink into this world!
> People wearing silk clothes,
> Buddhas dressed in rags,
> a wooden man walking in the evening,
> a stone woman with a bonnet—
> for the first time you will see,
> when you can cup your hands
> and pick up the moon as it floats
> on the still surface of a pond.

Sincerely yours,
S.S.

10. Not Difficult, Not Easy

In May, 1975, a student decided to move into the newly formed New Haven Zen Center. He wrote to a man with whom he had studied Zen and asked him what he thought of the decision. The Zen teacher wrote back at length and said, among other things, "Zen training is hard work. Make no mistake about this. There is no easy way. Dogen says, 'Those who seek the easy way do not seek the true way.' "

The student asked Seung Sahn Soen-sa for his advice. Soen-sa said, "If you want the easy way, this is desire. But if you want the difficult way, this too is desire. Zen is letting go of all your desires. Then you will find the true way.

"This teacher says that Zen is difficult. I say that Zen is very easy. But we are saying the same thing. Buddha said, 'All things have Buddha-nature.' Jo-ju, when he was asked if a dog has Buddha-nature, said, 'No!' Is Buddha right and Jo-ju wrong? These are just two different ways of teaching.

"Why do I teach that Zen is easy? Many Zen students in the United States have Difficulty Sickness. 'Oh, Zen is very difficult! We must do *zazen* and *sesshins* all the time. Then maybe in ten or twenty years we will attain enlightenment.' So when I show them that Zen is easy, I cure their attachment to difficulty. When Jo-ju was teaching, many students were attached to Buddha and Buddha-nature. So: 'Does the dog have Buddha-nature?' 'NO!!!!!!' This is Jo-ju's way.

"But if you think that Zen is difficult or easy, these words become a hindrance and you can't understand Zen. I always teach that if you are not thinking, just like this is Buddha. 'Difficult' is thinking; 'easy' is thinking. You mustn't be attached to words. If you are attached to Jo-ju's No, you can't understand Jo-ju's mind. If you are attached to my words, you can't understand my 'easy way.'

"Once there was a famous Buddhist layman named Busol. He was a deeply enlightened man; his wife too was enlightened, and so were his son and daughter. A man came up to Busol one day and asked, 'Is Zen difficult or not?' Busol said, 'Oh, it's very difficult. It's like taking a stick and trying to hit the moon.'

"The man was puzzled and began to think. 'If Zen is so difficult, how did Busol's wife attain enlightenment?' So he went and asked her the same question. She said, 'It's the easiest thing in the world. It's just like touching your nose when you wash your face in the morning.'

"By now the man was thoroughly confused. 'I don't understand. Is Zen easy? Is it difficult? Who is right?' So he asked their son. The son said, 'Zen is not difficult and not easy. On the tips of a hundred blades of grass is the Patriarchs' meaning.'

" 'Not difficult? Not easy? What is it then?' So the man went to the daughter and asked her. 'Your father, your mother, and your brother all gave me different answers. Who is right?' She said, 'If you make difficult, it is difficult. If you make easy, it is easy. But if you don't think, the truth is just as it is. Tell me now—how are you keeping your mind at this very moment?'

"The man was totally confused. Suddenly the daughter hit him and said, 'Where are difficult and easy now?' He understood.

"So you mustn't think that Zen is difficult or that it is easy. Zen is just as it is."

11. A Dharma Speech

Given by Seung Sahn Soen-sa
at the opening ceremony of the
International Zen Center
of New York on April 20, 1975.

(Holding up his Zen stick and hitting the table, slowly, three times)
Is this closed? Is this open?

If you say "closed," you fall into the hell without doors.
If you say "open," you are dancing with all demons.

Why?

(Holding up the Zen stick and tracing a circle in the air; then holding the stick perpendicular to the table) One two three four; five six seven eight.

(After a few moments) Thank you very much for coming to our ceremony even though you must be very busy. It is not an accident that we are gathered here today. It is the result of our past karma. It is very good karma that has brought us to meet here in front of the Buddha's altar.

This karma means finding our true self and attaining the Absolute. It means leaving behind the world of desire and journeying to the land of true freedom and peace.

That is why we founded Won Gak Sa one year ago and are opening the International Zen Center of New York today.

But the Sutra says, "Form is emptiness, emptiness is form." So all names and all forms are emptiness. Won Gak Sa, the International Zen Center of New York, this opening ceremony—these also are emptiness.

The Sutra says, "All beings are already Buddha." So why is chanting or reading sutras or sitting Zen necessary?

30

But we don't know ourselves. Desire, anger, and ignorance cover up our clear mind. If we cut off all thinking and return to empty mind, then your mind, my mind, and all people's minds are the same. We become one with the whole universe.

Therefore an eminent teacher said, "All things in the universe return to the One."

True empty mind is before thinking. So thinking does not appear and does not disappear. There is the realm where nothing appears or disappears.

In the realm where nothing appears or disappears, there is no life and no death, no suffering and no happiness, no good and no bad, no you and no I. So it is said that all things in the universe return to One.

But where does this One return?

Once somebody came up to the great Zen Master Mang Gong and asked him, "If all things return to the One, where does this One return?" Mang Gong said, "The spring geese are flying north."

What do you think this means—"The spring geese are flying north"?

Even though you may understand enough to smash Mount Sumeru into a million pieces and swallow the ocean in one gulp, you will not understand this.

Even though you may understand enough to kill or give life to all the Buddhas of the three time-worlds and all eminent teachers and all people, you will not begin to understand this.

Then how can you understand the true meaning of "The spring geese are flying north"? Only keep don't-know mind. This don't-know mind is the mind that is stuck and cannot budge. It is like trying to break through a steel wall or trying to climb a silver mountain. All thinking is cut off. But as soon as you penetrate this condition, your mind will explode. Then you can see the stone lion run across the waves and devour the sun.

But you will still be bewildered. Go one step further. Then you will arrive at your true home, where spring comes and the flowers are blossoming everywhere. If you arrive here, not only will sutras and bibles be true, but also the sound of water and wind, the color of the mountain, the barking of a dog in the street—everything that you see or sense, everything as it is, will be the truth.

Therefore Zen Master Mang Gong said, "The spring geese are flying north." The truth is just like this.

All things in the universe return to the One; where does the One return? Throw away Small I and enter Empty I. Then, when you open your eyes, everything that you can see and hear will be like this.

A little while ago I hit the table three times. Mang Gong said, "The spring geese are flying north." The meaning of my action and the meaning of Mang Gong's words—are these the same or different?

If you say "the same," I will hit you thirty times. If you say "different," I will still hit you thirty times.

Why?

KATZ!!!

Open the front door to Broadway.

12. What Is One Plus Two?

One day Seung Sahn Soen-sa asked his students, "What is one plus two?"

One student answered, "Three."

Soen-sa said, "Wrong. One plus two is zero."

"Why? If you add one apple to two apples, you have three apples."

"If I eat one apple and two apples, then there are no apples."

"That's not right."

"You say one plus two equals three. I say one plus two equals zero. Who is right?"

The student couldn't answer.

Soen-sa hit him and said, "The lion claws people; the dog runs after the bone."

The next day, Soen-sa again asked his students, "What is one plus two?"

One student shouted "KATZ!!!"

"Is this the truth?"

"No."

"Then what is the truth?"

"One plus two equals three."

Soen-sa said, "I thought you were a blind dog, but now I see you are a keen-eyed lion."

13. What to Do About Noise

One day a student at the Cambridge Zen Center said to Seung Sahn Soen-sa, "I am disturbed by noise when I sit Zen. What can I do about this?"

Soen-sa said, "What color is this rug?"

"Blue."

"Is it quiet or noisy?"

"Quiet."

"Who makes it quiet?"

The student shrugged his shoulders.

Soen-sa said, "You do. Noisy and quiet are made by your thinking. If you think something is noisy, it is noisy; if you think something is quiet, it is quiet. Noisy is not noisy, quiet is not quiet. True quiet is neither quiet nor noisy. If you listen to the traffic with a clear mind, without any concepts, it is not noisy, it is only what it is. Noisy and quiet are opposites. The Absolute is only like this."

There were a few moments of silence. Then Soen-sa said, "What is the opposite of blue?"

The student said, "I don't know."

Soen-sa said, "Blue is blue. White is white. This is the truth."

14. You Must Become *Completely* Crazy

One day a visitor came to the Providence Zen Center and asked Seung Sahn Soen-sa, "If I study Zen, will I attain enlightenment?"

Soen-sa said, "Why do you want to attain enlightenment?"

The visitor said, "I'm upset by all sorts of things. I don't feel free."

Soen-sa said, "Why don't you feel free?"

"I guess I have too many attachments."

"Why don't you cut through these attachments?"

"They all seem very real."

Soen-sa said, "No one knows when he will die. It could be next year, or next week, or in the next five minutes. So put it all down, now, at this very moment. Keep your mind as if you were already dead. Then all your attachments will disappear, and it won't matter whether you study Zen or not. Right now you think, 'I am alive, I am strong.' So you have many desires, many attachments. Only think, 'I am dead.' A dead man has no desires."

The visitor said, "How can I be alive and dead?"

Soen-sa said, "Dead is not dead. We have eyes, ears, nose, tongue, body, and mind. But the Heart Sutra says that in emptiness there are no eyes, no ears, no nose, no tongue, no body, no mind. Without my six senses I have no hindrance. It is very easy. So if I am already dead, seeing is not seeing, hearing is not hearing. It is like passing in front of a restaurant, smelling the good smells, and passing on. It is not my house, so I don't touch."

The visitor said, "How can I practice being dead?"

Soen-sa said, "Only keep the great question, 'What am I?' Now let me ask you, what are you?"

"I'm one."

"Where does one come from?"

"From God. God is one."

"God? Do you understand God?"

"No."

"You say 'one,' you say 'God.' This is wrong. If you make one, it is one. If you make God, it is God. All this is thinking. Without thinking, what are you?"

"Nothing."

"Nothing?" Soen-sa hit him and said, "This is pain. Can 'nothing' feel pain?"

The visitor smiled.

Soen-sa said, "Before thinking, your mind was like a sheet of white paper. Then you wrote down 'one,' and 'God,' and 'nothing,' and so on and so forth. When you cut off all thinking, you erase all these names and forms and return to your original emptiness. What am I? I don't know. When you keep the great question, you keep the mind that doesn't know. Don't-know mind is empty mind. There are no words, no speech. So there is no one, no God, no nothing, no mind, no emptiness. This don't-know mind is very important. I is don't-know, don't-know is I. Only this. This is your true self. So always keep don't-know mind."

The visitor said, "My friends think I'm crazy because I'm interested in Zen."

Soen-sa said, "Craziness is good. Crazy people are happy, free, they have no hindrance. But since you have many attachments, you are only a little crazy. This is not crazy enough. You must become *completely* crazy. Then you will understand."

The visitor bowed. Someone came and poured out two cups of tea.

15. The Story of Ko Bong

Ko Bong was one of the greatest Zen Masters in Sung dynasty China.

When he was twenty years old, his teacher gave him the kong-an: "Where was I before I was born, and where will I be after I die?" As he meditated on this kong-an, he came to feel like a traveler who had lost his way in a dark forest. "At that time," he later wrote, "I was altogether dazed by my own delusions."

Three years passed. Ko Bong struggled with the kong-an day and night, unable to achieve any degree of one-pointedness. Finally, in despair, he went to see the famous Zen Master Seorl Am. Ko Bong told him of his failure to penetrate the kong-an, and asked for his help.

"We have been told," said the Master, "that all beings have Buddha-nature. This is the teaching of all Buddhas, past, present, and future. However, when a monk came to

Zen Master Jo-ju and asked if dogs have Buddha-nature, Jo-ju said, 'No!' What does this 'No' mean?"

Ko Bong was stunned. As he struggled to come up with an answer, the Master took his staff, hit him viciously on the shoulder, and chased him out.

So, in great pain, and weeping with humiliation, Ko Bong returned to his monastery. He couldn't stop thinking about the Master's question. What could it mean? What could it mean? Suddenly, like a flame in a dark room, an understanding was kindled inside his mind, and it spread until it filled his whole being. The original kong-an—"Where was I before I was born, and where will I be after I die?"—seemed obvious now.

The next day, as he was working in the monastery fields, Seorl Am came to visit. He said, "Good morning. How is your search coming along?"

Ko Bong said, "If a man kills his desire to search, he will surely find what he is searching for."

Suddenly the Master grabbed him by the collar and shouted, "Who is dragging this corpse?" Although Ko Bong had understood the kong-an perfectly, he again was paralyzed and could only stare like a moron. The Master pushed him away and left.

Ko Bong was so troubled by this new failure that he couldn't sleep for days. Then, one night, his first teacher appeared to him in a dream and gave him another kong-an: "All things return to the One; where does the One return?" When he woke up, he found that all his doubts and confusion has coalesced into one mass, which weighed on his heart like a huge rock. For five days he walked about in a stupor. On the sixth day he wandered into the great hall of the monastery, where the monks happened to be commemorating the death of the fifth patriarch of the Lin-chi school. For the occasion, they had hung up a portrait of the patriarch, on which he himself had inscribed the following stanza:

> Thirty-six thousand mornings
> in one hundred years.
> Don't you know by now
> that it is the same old fellow?

As Ko Bong read the last word, a realization burst upon him. "At that moment," he later wrote, "I felt as if the whole universe had been chopped up into tiny pieces and the whole earth leveled flat. There was no I, there was no world. It was like one mirror reflecting another. I asked myself several kong-ans, and the answers were transparently clear."

The next day he went to see Seorl Am. The Master asked him, "Who is dragging around this lifeless body of yours?"

Ko Bong shouted "KATZ!!!"

The Master took hold of his stick, but Ko Bong snatched it out of his hand and said, "Uh-uh. You can't hit me today."

The Master said, "Why not?"

Ko Bong got up and walked out of the room.

Some time later, another Zen Master visited Ko Bong and said, "Congratulations, I hear you have attained the great enlightenment."

Ko Bong smiled and said, "Thank you."

The Master said, "Can you maintain this state at all times?"

"Yes indeed."

"While you are working or sleeping or dreaming?"

"Yes, even in dreams."

"How about in dreamless sleep, where there is no sight or sound or consciousness. Where is your enlightenment then?"

Seeing that Ko Bong couldn't answer, the Master said, "Let me give you some advice. When you are hungry, eat; when you are tired, rest. The minute you wake up every morning, ask yourself, 'Who is the master of this body, and where does he reside?' This will lead you to a final understanding."

So Ko Bong made up his mind to work on this question without interruption, even if it should drive him insane.

Five years passed.

Then he and a friend left on a pilgrimage to the north of China. On their way they stopped at an inn. Being very tired, the friend fell asleep immediately. Ko Bong sat in a corner and meditated. Suddenly, as the friend moved in his sleep, his wooden pillow fell to the floor. Ko Bong heard the noise and his mind burst open and the whole universe was flooded with light. He understood not only his own kong-an, but all the kong-ans handed down by Buddha and the patriarchs. He felt like a distant traveler who has finally come home. At this moment of great awakening, he composed the following stanza:

> The man who has come to this
> is the man who was here from the beginning.
> He does what he always did.
> Nothing has changed.

16. How Can the Buddha Be Smiling?

May 5, 1973

Dear Soen-sa-nim,

Tonight was Special Zen. No one was sleeping. When we finished, Alban walked around with the stick and hit everyone very hard. Good Zen Master. Tonight we had five customers; sometimes we have none.

My father wants more *kim-chee*.

Today I went to many stores and bought a lot of food. You are not here—no good. I like you to help me.

I hope you are well. Everyone here is okay. We eat a lot, sit Zen a lot, say mantras, think a lot. Spring is here, the flowers are blooming. The Buddha is smiling.

Bobby

May 14, 1973

Dear Bobby,

Thank you for your letter, books, and pictures. So far I am very well. We had a wonderful ceremony on Buddha's birthday. More than two hundred people attended.

I am very glad to hear that everyone in Providence is sitting Zen earnestly and that Alban is doing a good job as Zen Master. I am always thinking and worrying about you, because you have a hard job taking care of everyone at the Zen Center. But I know you are doing very well. I will be back as soon as I can to help you.

You said, "We eat a lot, sit Zen a lot, say mantras, think a lot." This is a very fine sentence. But I have one question for you: Were these actions done inside your mind or outside it?

Your next sentences were also very fine. But:

1) Originally everything is empty. Where does spring come from?

2) The real Buddha has no name or form. How can the Buddha be smiling?

Now if you answer, I will hit you thirty times. And if you don't answer, I will still hit you thirty times.

Why?

> A wooden chicken is swimming in the water.
> A stone fish is playing in the sky.
> Form-body and karma-body come from thinking.
> Dharma-body is pure and clear and infinite
>   in time and space.
> On the water of a thousand rivers,
>   a thousand moons are reflected.
> There are no clouds over ten thousand miles,
>   only blue sky for ten thousand miles.

See you soon.
S.S.

17. Apples and Oranges

One day Seung Sahn Soen-sa was sitting in the kitchen of the Providence Zen Center with some of his students. In the center of the table was a bowl filled with apples and oranges. He picked up an apple and said, "What is this?"

One student said, "Don't you know?"

Soen-sa said, "I'm asking *you*."

The student said, "It's an apple."

Soen-sa then picked up an orange and said, "This apple and this orange—are they the same or different?"

The student took the apple and bit into it.

Soen-sa said, "Does this apple have Buddha-nature?"

"No."

"Why not? The Buddha said that all things have Buddha-nature. You say that this apple doesn't have Buddha-nature. Which one is the truth?"

The student handed the apple to Soen-sa.

"I don't want this apple. Give me another answer."

"The apple is red."

Soen-sa said, "Before, I didn't know what color the apple was. But now that you tell me, I know that it is red."

18. Kong-an Blues

March 4, 1975

Dear Soen-sa-nim,

Enclosed you will find an assortment of letters I have written and never mailed to you, so here they are.

My practice is I don't know what. It is neither good nor bad, I guess, but still I don't know what. It seems I don't know what about anything, which seems different from I don't know what.

Tell me about shakuhachi practice. It is my ego that wants to play well. How can I just play? As I watch my playing I sense today that all things are like those music notes on the page. It says: move third finger. How can I learn to live each moment as when each note directs me and fulfill that request as best I can? I don't really know what I am saying but I must write you and I hope I mail these letters to you.

See Hoy

March 5, 1975

Dear Soen-sa-nim,

I am very confused. Since you are not here I go to sit with Venerable Hearn and sometimes Dr. Thien-An. Venerable

Hearn is here only once a week for *dokusan* and will be leaving for the Asian countries at the end of the month.

Once, soon after you went to Providence, I went to visit with Roshi Kozan Kimura. Here are a list of *kong-ans* given to me:

From you: "What am I?"

"Why does Bodhidharma have no beard?"

From Venerable Hearn: "What is the sound of the flute with no holes?"

One day he said to me, "Now show me your understanding of this," and gave me the *kong-an*, "Can you drive a nail without a hammer?"

Dr. Thien-An: "Where do you find Buddha-nature?"

My answer: "Galloping through, it is all around. How could it leave a trace?"

He said: "Go work on it some more."

Kimura Roshi said I should decide on one Master. I told him you were not here. He told me I should follow you around and go to Providence. He said he likes me to come and sit Zen with them but would not give me *dokusan* lest he interfere with another's *kong-an*.

Last night I went to sit with him and had no *dokusan*. Tonight I went to sit and went to *dokusan*. He said I should only work on one *kong-an* and asked me to meditate on "When were you born?" After all others were finished with *dokusan*, I went back and answered with, "Since there is no trace, how should I know?" We then talked and he asked me what other *kong-ans* I had and which I worked on. I told him I work most on "What am I?" He said it is too hard for beginners and I should work on "When were you born?"

Please advise me, because when I sit Zen I can only ask —rather, I like only to ask—"What am I?" and even at other times only "What am I?" I do not know what to do.

Shall I just go and sit with Kozan but have no *dokusan*? Shall I come to Providence? But here I have so many attachments and even to you attachment.

Sometimes I remember you asking "What am I?" and can even get angry with you for giving me such a thing.

Even now I am attached to "What am I?" and the thought

of "When was I born?" makes me want to vomit, because all these things are puzzling my head. I will sit more *zazen* tonight and only think "What am I?" Please help me because I think only you can take "What am I?" back.

Please answer me soon, but you probably won't, huh? Anyway, I'd like to tell you to go fuck yourself.

Respectfully, and hope to see you soon,

See Hoy

March 22, 1975

Dear See Hoy,

Thank you for your two letters. I have been in New York since the beginning of the month, so I didn't receive them until a few days ago. That's why my answer is so late. I am sorry.

You say that you don't know what your practice is, that you don't know anything. But then you say that you are confused. If you keep a complete don't-know mind, how can confusion appear? Complete don't-know mind means cutting off all thinking. Cutting off all thinking means true emptiness. In true emptiness, there is no I to be confused and nothing to be confused about. True emptiness is before thinking. Before thinking, everything does not appear and does not disappear. So the truth is just like this. Red comes, there is red; white comes, there is white. When you close all the holes of the shakuhachi, there is no sound; when the holes are open, there is a high sound. Only like this. The shakuhachi is a very good teacher for you. If you don't understand, just ask the shakuhachi. Just enter the sound of the shakuhachi, and the shakuhachi will explain to you what enlightenment is.

Dr. Thien-An, Song Ryong Hearn, and Kimura Roshi are all good teachers. I think you can take your questions and problems to any of them and they will teach you well.

You have many *kong-ans.* But a *kong-an* is like a finger pointing at the moon. If you are attached to the finger, you don't understand the direction, so you cannot see the moon. If you are not attached to any *kong-an,* then you will understand the direction. The direction is the complete don't-know mind. The name for "like this" is "don't know." If you understand "don't know," you will understand all *kong-ans* and you will soon understand "like this."

You have many problems in your *kong-an* work. "What am I?"—do you understand this? Your answer is, "I don't know." "When were you born?"—do you understand this? Your answer is also, "I don't know." If you are not attached to words, the don't-know mind is the same. All *kong-ans* become the same don't-know mind. Your don't-know mind, my don't-know mind, all people's don't-know minds, the "What am I?" don't-know mind, the "When was I born?" don't-know mind—all these are the same don't-know. So it is very easy. Only keep don't-know. Don't be attached to words. This don't-know is your true self. It is nothing at all. It is very easy, not difficult.

So you must keep only don't-know, always and every-where. Then you will soon get enlightenment. But be very careful not to want enlightenment. Only keep don't-know mind.

Your situation, your condition, your opinions—throw them all away.

I think it would be very good for you to learn with Kimura Roshi. I hope you also listen to what your shakuhachi is teaching you and soon get enlightenment.

At the end of your letter you say, "Go fuck yourself." These are wonderful words that you have given me, and I thank you very much. If you attain enlightenment, I will give them back to you.

Sincerely yours,
S. S.

19. The 84,000 Levels of Enlightenment

One Thursday evening, after a Dharma talk at the Cambridge Zen Center, a student said to Seung Sahn Soen-sa, "I have a question about enlightenment. Now enlightenment is very good . . ."

Soen-sa said, "It is very bad!" (Laughter from the audience.)

The student said, "The perfected virtues of enlightenment were outlined by the Lord Buddha himself. He said that enlightenment has seven limbs."

"Seven?"

"Seven."

"No—many more than that!" (Laughter.)

"My question is, if one has awakened, is that enough? Is Anuttara Samyak Sambodhi, the Unexcelled Perfect Enlightenment, enough? Is that the same as Nirvana? Or is Nirvana a provisional form? Some teachers say there are two levels of enlightenment, some say there are three. What do you teach about levels of enlightenment? Are there one, two, three, or more?"

Soen-sa said, "There are many levels of enlightenment. About 84,000 levels. How many do you want?" (Laughter.)

"That's very interesting."

"I will teach you all of them." (Laughter.)

"I've heard this teaching before. This comes from T'ien-t'ai philosophy."

"How many do you want? One, two, three, 84,000?"

"I'm aware of the teaching. But could you describe what are the two stages ..."

Soen-sa handed the student a cup of water and said, "Drink this."

The student drank.

"How did it taste?"

"As water should."

"You have just attained the 84,000 levels of enlightenment." (Laughter.)

The student said, "That's more than I expected." (Laughter.) "Thank you."

Soen-sa said, "Okay, now I will explain. In Zen, we teach that there are three kinds of enlightenment." Then, holding up the *moktak**, "This is a *moktak*. But if you say it is a *moktak*, you are attached to name and form. And if you say it is not a *moktak*, you are attached to emptiness. So is this a *moktak* or not? This is one of the elementary *kong-ans* that we use. If you answer by hitting the floor or shouting 'KATZ!!!' or hitting me, this is first enlightenment. Everything becomes one. Buddha, you, me, the *moktak*, the sound, KATZ, HIT—all becomes one. The ten thousand dharmas return to the One."

The student snapped his fingers.

"That's correct. This is first enlightenment. Next is original enlightenment. Is this a *moktak* or not? This time, you answer, 'The wall is white, the *moktak* is brown,' or, 'The sky is blue, the grass is green,' or, 'Three times three equals nine.' Everything is like this. This is original enlightenment. Okay?"

"Okay."

"Next is final enlightenment. This is very important. What is final enlightenment?" Soen-sa hit the *moktak*. "Only this. Only one point. The truth is just like this. So we teach that there are three kinds: first enlightenment, original enlightenment, and final enlightenment. At first they seem to be the same. But they are not the same. Is it clear now?"

"Much clearer than usual."

---

*A gourd-like instrument used to set the rhythm during chanting.

"Only this. If you do hard training in Zen, you will soon understand."

"Thank you."

"Okay, then I ask you: Once Zen Master Dong Sahn was weighing flax. Somebody came up to him and asked, 'What is Buddha?' He answered, 'Three pounds of flax.' What does this mean?"

The student thought for a few moments, then said, "Three pounds of flax means just what three pounds of flax are."

Soen-sa said, "Only this?"

"That's all I can think of tonight."

"Yah, that's a good answer. Not bad, not good."

The student was silent.

Soen-sa said, "Okay, next question. Somebody asked Zen Master Un-mun, 'What is Buddha?' Un-mun answered, 'Dry shit on a stick.' Both Zen Masters were asked, 'What is Buddha?' But Dong Sahn said, 'Three pounds of flax' and Un-mun said, 'Dry shit on a stick.' Are these two answers the same or different?"

The student said, "When you understand with the one mind, they're the same."

Soen-sa said, "Only this?"

"It's the best I can do."

"I thought you were a keen-eyed lion, but now I understand that you are a blind dog."

The student said, "Maybe some day I'll be able to see."

Soen-sa said, "Now you are a blind dog. You must again become a keen-eyed lion."

The student closed his eyes and bowed.

20. What Is Freedom?

One afternoon, a young student came to tea at the Cambridge Zen Center and asked Seung Sahn Soen-sa, "What is freedom?"

Soen-sa said, "Freedom means no hindrance. If your parents tell you to do something and you think that you are a free person so you will not listen to them, this is not true freedom. True freedom is freedom from thinking, freedom from all attachments, freedom even from life and death. If I want life, I have life; if I want death, I have death."

The student said, "So if you wanted to die right now, you could die?"

Soen-sa said, "What is death?"

"I don't know."

"If you make death, there is death. If you make life, there is life. Do you understand? This is freedom. Freedom thinking is freedom. Attachment thinking is hindrance. Suppose your parents say, 'Your shirt is dirty; you must change it!' If you say, 'No, I won't change; I am free!', then you are attached to your dirty shirt or to your freedom itself. So you are not free. If you are really free, then dirty is good and clean is good. It doesn't matter. Not changing my shirt is good; changing my shirt is good. If my parents want me to change, then I change. I don't do it for my own sake, only for theirs. This is freedom. No desire for myself, only for all people."

The student said, "If you have no desire, why do you eat?"

Soen-sa said, "When I am hungry, I eat."

"But *why* do you eat, if you say you have no desire?"

"I eat for you."

"What do you mean?"

" 'When I am hungry, I eat' means 'just like this.' This means that there is no attachment to food. There is no 'I want this' or 'I don't want this.' If I didn't eat, I couldn't teach you. So I eat for you."

"I don't really understand."

Soen-sa hit him and said, "Do you understand now?"

"I don't know."

"You must understand this don't-know. Then you will not be attached to anything. So always keep don't-know mind. This is true freedom."

21. The Great Treasure

When Dae Ju first came to Zen Master Ma-jo, the Master asked him, "What do you want from me?"

Dae Ju said, "I want you to teach me the Dharma."

"What a fool you are!" said Ma-jo. "You have the greatest treasure in the world within you, and yet you go around asking other people for help. What good is this? I have nothing to give you."

Dae Ju bowed and said, "Please, Master, tell me what this treasure is."

Ma-jo said, "Where is your question coming from? *This* is your treasure. It is precisely what is making you ask the question at this very moment. Everything is stored in this precious treasure-house of yours. It is there at your disposal, you can use it as you wish, nothing is lacking. You are the master of everything. Why, then, are you running away from yourself and seeking for things outside?"

Upon hearing these words, Dae Ju attained enlightenment.

22. The Moon of Clear Mind

One Sunday evening, after a Dharma talk at the Providence Zen Center, a student asked Seung Sahn Soen-sa, "How can I get beyond just verbalizing the question 'What am I?'"

Soen-sa said, "You want this question to grow. This mind is no good. This is attachment thinking. You must cut off this thinking, and only do hard training. It is not important for the question to grow. What is important is one moment of clear mind. Clear mind is before thinking. If you experience this mind, you have already attained enlightenment. If you experience this for a short time—even for one moment—this is enlightenment. All the rest of the time you may be thinking, but you shouldn't worry about this thinking. It is just your karma. You must not be attached to this thinking. You must not force it to stop or force clear mind to grow. It will grow by itself, as your karma gradually disappears.

"Clear mind is like the full moon in the sky. Sometimes

clouds come and cover it, but the moon is always behind them. Clouds go away, then the moon shines brightly. So don't worry about clear mind: it is always there. When thinking comes, behind it is clear mind. When thinking goes, there is only clear mind. Thinking comes and goes, comes and goes. You must not be attached to the coming or the going."

23. What Have You Brought Here?

One Sunday morning, a student came into the interview room at the Providence Zen Center and bowed to Seung Sahn Soen-sa. Soen-sa said, "What have you brought here?"

The student hit the floor.

Soen-sa said, "Is this the truth?"

The student again hit the floor.

Soen-sa said, "You understand One; you don't understand Two."

The student hit the floor again.

Soen-sa said, "A second offense is not permitted."

The student bowed and left.

The next student came into the room. Soen-sa said, "What have you brought here?"

The student said, "I don't know."

Soen-sa said, "How long have you been sitting Zen?"

The student said, "Three months."

Soen-sa said, "Why do you sit Zen?"

"I think too much. I like the quietness."

Soen-sa said, "Where does your thinking come from?"

"I don't know."

Soen-sa said, "This don't-know mind cuts off all thinking, and is the true quiet mind. So ask yourself, 'What am I?' all the time, and keep your don't-know mind."

The student said, "Thank you very much."

Soen-sa said, "Next time, bring your don't-know mind here."

The student bowed and left.

Many students came and went. One student came and Soen-sa said, "What have you brought here?"

The student shouted "KATZ!!!"

Soen-sa put his hands over his ears and said, "Your KATZ has broken my ears."

The student again shouted "KATZ!!!"

Soen-sa asked, "Is KATZ all you brought here?"

The student said, "No."

Soen-sa said, "Then give me something else."

The student stood up, bowed, and said, "Did you sleep well last night?"

Soen-sa said, "Pretty well, thank you. Now go drink tea."

The student left.

The next student came. Soen-sa said, "What have you brought here?"

The student hit the floor. Soen-sa said, "Is this the truth?"

The student said, "No."

Soen-sa asked, "What is the truth?"

The student said, "Today is Sunday, July 22, 1973."

Soen-sa opened his *kong-an* book, and said, "Long ago a Zen Master said, 'When you hear a wooden chicken crow, you will understand your mind.' What does this mean?"

The student said, "A stone girl dances to the music of a flute with no holes."

Soen-sa said, "Not bad. Now, one more question for you. A person comes to the Providence Zen Center smoking a cigarette and blows smoke and drops ashes on the Buddha. If you are the Zen Master, what can you do?"

The student said, "I would hit him."

"This person is very strong. He only understands that he is Buddha, he is Dharma. He will hit you back."

The student said, "I would only sit."

Soen-sa said, "You are a Zen Master. You understand that he has an attachment to emptiness. If you only sit, you won't be teaching him."

The student said, "I'm not a Zen Master. So how would I know?"

The student and Soen-sa laughed together. Soen-sa said, "You must practice hard. I hope you soon attain enlightenment."

The student said, "Thank you very much," bowed, and left.

24. Enlightened and Unenlightened Are Empty Names

One Thursday evening, after a Dharma talk at the Cambridge Zen Center, a student asked Seung Sahn Soen-sa, "Is an enlightened man's behavior different from an unenlightened man's?"

Soen-sa said, "One, two, three, four, five, six. This begins with one. Where does one come from?"

"Mind."

"Mind? Where does mind come from?"

The student couldn't answer.

Soen-sa said, "Now your mind is don't-know mind. You only don't know. Where does mind come from? What is mind? I don't know. This don't-know is your true mind. This true mind cuts off all thinking. So mind is no mind. Why?

True mind is empty mind. Empty mind is before thinking. Before thinking there are no words and no speech. So mind is no mind. Mind is only a name; it is made by thinking. If you cut off thinking, then there is no mind. If you are thinking, you have opposites: good and bad, enlightened and unenlightened. But if you cut off thinking, there are no opposites, there is only the Absolute. Opposites words are dead words. Absolute words are live words. Buddha said, 'All things have Buddha-nature.' But Zen Master Jo-ju, when somebody asked him if a dog has Buddha-nature, said, 'No!' Which answer is correct, Buddha's or Jo-ju's?"

"I think I see that. They're just words."

"Yah, just words. Then they are the same?"

"It doesn't matter. But what I want to know is how a man with empty mind differs in his behavior from a man with thinking mind."

"So I ask you: are Buddha's answer and Jo-ju's answer different or the same?"

"Well, all things have Buddha-nature. Some people know they have Buddha-nature and some people don't know they have Buddha-nature. Maybe the dog doesn't know."

Soen-sa said, "That is a very good answer. The dog doesn't know Buddha-nature, so he has no Buddha-nature. But if you gave me this answer during an interview, I would hit you thirty times. Why?"

"Uh . . . I'm not answering to play a game."

"And if you asked your question about an enlightened man's behavior during an interview, I would also hit you thirty times. Do you understand?"

" I understand that this question has no answer."

"It has many answers." (Laughter from the audience.) "But if you have not attained enlightenment, everything is different. If you attain enlightenment, all things become one. You must understand this."

The student bowed and said, "Thank you very much."

25. Why We Chant

One Sunday evening, after a Dharma talk at the International Zen Center of New York, a student asked Seung Sahn Soen-sa, "Why do you chant? Isn't sitting Zen enough?"

Soen-sa said, "This is a very important matter. We bow together, chant together, eat together, sit together, and do many other things together here at the Zen Center. Why do we practice together?

"Everybody has different karma. So all people have different situations, different conditions, and different opinions. One person is a monk, another is a student, another works in a factory; one person always keeps a clear mind, another is often troubled or dissatisfied; one person likes the women's movement, another doesn't. But everybody thinks, '*My* opinion is correct!' Even Zen Masters are like this. Ten Zen Masters will have ten different ways of teaching, and each Zen Master will think that his way is the best. Americans have an American opinion; Orientals have an Oriental opinion. Different opinions result in different actions, which make different karma. So when you hold on to your own opinions, it is very difficult to control your karma, and your life will remain difficult. Your wrong opinions continue, so your bad karma continues. But at our Zen Centers, we live together and practice together, and all of us abide by the Temple Rules. People come to us with many strong likes and dislikes, and gradually cut them all off. Everybody bows together 108 times at five-thirty in the morning, everybody sits together, everybody eats together, everybody works together. Sometimes you don't feel like bowing; but this is a temple rule, so you bow. Sometimes you don't want to chant, but you chant. Sometimes you are tired and want to sleep; but you know that if you don't come to sitting, people will wonder why; so you sit.

"When we eat, we eat in ritual style, with four bowls; and after we finish eating, we wash out the bowls with tea, using our index finger to clean them. The first few times we ate this way, nobody liked it. One person from the Cambridge Zen Center came to me very upset. 'I can't stand this way of eating! The tea gets full of garbage! I can't drink it!' I said to him, 'Do you know the Heart Sutra?' 'Yes.' 'Doesn't it say that things are neither tainted nor pure?' 'Yes.' 'Then why can't you drink the tea?' 'Because it's filthy!' " (Laughter from the audience.) " 'Why is it filthy? These crumbs are from the food that you already ate. If you think the tea is dirty, it is dirty. If you think it is clean, it is clean.' He said, 'You're right. I will drink the tea.' " (Laughter.)

"So we live together and act together. Acting together means cutting off my opinions, cutting off my condition, cutting off my situation. Then we become empty mind. We return to white paper. Then our true opinion, our true condition, our true situation will appear. When we bow together and chant together and eat together, our minds become one mind. It is like on the sea. When the wind comes, there are many waves. When the wind dies down, the waves become smaller. When the wind stops, the water becomes a mirror, in which everything is reflected—mountains, trees, clouds. Our mind is the same. When we have many desires and many opinions, there are many big waves. But after we sit Zen and act together for some time, our opinions and desires disappear. The waves become smaller and smaller. Then our mind is like a clear mirror, and everything we see or hear or smell or taste or touch or think is the truth. Then it is very easy to understand other people's minds. Their minds are reflected in my mind.

"So chanting is very important. At first you won't understand. But after you chant regularly, you will understand.

'Ah, chanting—very good feeling!' It is the same with bowing 108 times. At first people don't like this. Why do we bow? We are not bowing to Buddha, we are bowing to ourselves. Small I is bowing to Big I. Then Small I disappears and becomes Big I. This is true bowing. So come practice with us. You will soon understand."

The student bowed and said, "Thank you very much."

26. A Dharma Speech

On the Buddha's birthday, 1973, Seung Sahn Soen-sa gave the following Dharma speech at the Providence Zen Center:

"Long ago an eminent teacher said, 'Before the Buddha came to the Kapila Empire or was born of his mother, he had already saved all people from suffering.'

"This is having a thousand mouths, and yet not needing them. If you understand this, then you will understand that in the palm of your hand you hold the noses of all the eminent teachers from the distant past to the present. So you will first attain. If you do not understand, you should not speak, for that is only blood dripping. It is better for you to keep your mouth shut as spring passes.

"The Buddha sprang from the right side of his mother and took seven steps in each of the four directions. He then looked once each way, pointed one finger to the sky, and touched the ground with his other hand. He said, 'In the sky above and the sky below, only I am holy.'

"You must understand this speech and understand what

this 'I' is. 'I' is empty. Empty is full. It has no name or form, and does not appear or disappear. All people and all things have it. So where does the Buddha come from?

"Long ago Zen Master Un-mun said, 'On the Buddha's birthday, as he sprang from the side of his mother, I hit him once and killed him, and fed him to a hungry dog. The whole world was at peace.'

"What the Buddha said on his birthday is wrong, so I will hit him thirty times. What Zen Master Un-mun said is also wrong, so I will hit him thirty times. What I just said is wrong, so I will hit myself thirty times.

"Where is the mistake?

"KATZ!!!

"Today is the Buddha's birthday, and outside white snow is falling."

After the Dharma speech, Soen-sa asked if there were any questions.

One student said, "Some people say the Buddha is a divine being, others say he was super-human, others say he was just a wise old man who understood a little more than most people. Who is Buddha?"

Soen-sa said, "How did you get here?"

"I walked."

"Why did you walk?"

"I don't have a car."

"A person drives a car. What is it that drove your body here?"

"I don't know."

"The mind that doesn't know is the Buddha."

"Then why do you celebrate Buddha's birthday?"

"Zen Master Un-mun said, 'On the Buddha's birthday, as he sprang from the side of his mother, I hit him once and killed him, and fed him to a hungry dog. The whole world was at peace.' Do you understand what this means?"

"No."

"This is the Buddha's teaching. When you understand it, you will understand why we celebrate his birthday."

27. The Story of Won Hyo

Thirteen hundred years ago, in an ancient province of Korea, there was a great Zen Master named Won Hyo. As a young man, he fought in a bloody civil war and saw many friends slaughtered and homes destroyed. He was overcome by the emptiness of this life, so he shaved his head and went to the mountains to live the life of a monk. In the mountains he read many sutras and kept the precepts well, but still he didn't understand the true meaning of Buddhism. Finally, since he knew that in China he might find a Zen Master who could help him become enlightened, he put on his backpack and headed for the great dry northern plains.

He went on foot. He would walk all day long and rest at night. One evening, as he was crossing the desert, he stopped at a small patch of green, where there were a few trees and some water, and went to sleep. Toward midnight he woke up, very thirsty. It was pitch-dark. He groped along on all fours, searching for water. At last his hand touched a cup on the ground. He picked it up and drank. Ah, how delicious! Then he bowed deeply, in gratitude to Buddha for the gift of water.

The next morning, Won Hyo woke up and saw beside him what he had taken for a cup. It was a shattered skull, blood-caked and with shreds of flesh still stuck to the cheek-bones. Strange insects crawled or floated on the surface of the filthy rain-water inside it. Won Hyo looked at the skull and felt a great wave of nausea. He opened his mouth. As soon as the vomit poured out, his mind opened and he understood. Last night, since he hadn't seen and hadn't thought, the water was delicious. This morning, seeing and thinking had made him vomit. Ah, he said to himself, thinking makes good and bad, life and death. It creates the whole universe. It is the universal master. And without thinking, there is no universe, no Buddha, no Dharma. All is one, and this one is empty.

There was no need now to find a Master. Won Hyo already understood life and death. What more was there to learn? So he turned and started back across the desert to Korea.

Twenty years passed. During this time Won Hyo became the most famous monk in the land. He was the trusted advisor of the great king of Shilla, and preceptor to the noblest and most powerful families. Whenever he gave a public lecture, the hall was packed. He lived in a beautiful temple, taught the best students, ate the best food, and slept the dreamless sleep of the just.

Now at this time, there was a very great Zen Master in Shilla—a little old man, with a wisp of a beard and skin like a crumpled paper bag. Barefoot and in tattered clothes, he would walk through the towns ringing his bell. *De-an, * de-an, de-an, de-an don't think, de-an like this, de-an rest mind, de-an, de-an.* Won Hyo heard of him and one day hiked to the mountain cave where he lived. From a distance he could hear the sound of extraordinarily lovely chanting echoing through the valleys. But when he arrived at the cave, he found the Master sitting beside a dead fawn, weeping. Won Hyo was dumbfounded. How could an enlightened being be either happy or sad, since in the state of Nirvana there is nothing to be happy or sad about, and no one to be happy or sad? He stood speechless for a while, and then asked the Master why he was weeping.

The Master explained. He had come upon the fawn after its mother had been killed by hunters. It was very hungry. So he had gone into town and begged for milk. Since he

---

*This means, in Chinese, "The Great Peace."

knew that no one would give milk for an animal, he had said it was for his son. "A monk with a son? What a dirty old man!" people thought. But some gave him a little milk. He had continued this way for a month, begging enough to keep the animal alive. Then the scandal became too great, and no one would help. He had been wandering for three days now, in search of milk. At last he had found some, but when he had returned to the cave, his fawn was already dead. "You don't understand," said the Master. "My mind and the fawn's mind are the same. It was very hungry. I want milk, I want milk. Now it is dead. Its mind is my mind. That's why I am weeping. I want milk."

Won Hyo began to understand how great a Bodhisattva the Master was. When all creatures were happy, he was happy. When all creatures were sad, he was sad. He said to him, "Please teach me." The Master said, "All right. Come along with me."

They went to the red-light district of town. The Master took Won Hyo's arm and walked up to the door of a geisha-house. *De-an, de-an,* he rang. A beautiful woman opened the door. "Today I've brought the great monk Won Hyo to visit you." "Oh! Won Hyo!" she cried out. Won Hyo blushed. The woman blushed, and her eyes grew large. She led them upstairs, in great happiness, fear, and exhilaration that the famous, handsome monk had come to her. As she prepared meat and wine for her visitors, the Master said to Won Hyo, "For twenty years you've kept company with kings and princes and monks. It's not good for a monk to live in heaven all the time. He must also visit hell and save the people there, who are wallowing in their desires. Hell too is 'like this.' So tonight you will ride this wine straight to hell."

"But I've never broken a single Precept before," Won Hyo said.

"Have a good trip," said the Master.

He then turned to the woman and said sternly, "Don't you know it's a sin to give wine to a monk? Aren't you afraid of going to hell?"

"No," the woman said. "Won Hyo will come and save me."

"A very good answer!" said the Master.

So Won Hyo stayed the night, and broke more than one Precept. The next morning he took off his elegant robes and went dancing through the streets, barefoot and in tatters. *"De-an, de-an, de-an!* The whole universe is like this! What are you?"

28. Porcupines in Rat-Holes

August 10, 1974

Dear Soen-sa-nim,

Thank you for your most recent "hit"—my humble apologies for soiling this almost clean white paper with thinking, and even thinking about thinking.

My overall state is very good. Teaching here in Boulder is the best it has ever been for me—the tremendous enthusiasm, hunger, and sincerity of the students helps me rise beyond myself at times. My practice continues (I bow 108 times to the Cambridge Zen Center each morning) and my health flourishes. My first real exposure to real mountains is beyond words. I try to get to my favorite spot, near a glacier lake 10,000 feet high. "What am I?" at 10,000 feet!!!! At times I am a bit lonely for you all. Rinpoche is a Tantric master— there is much drinking, sex, drugs, etc. Ten years ago this might have been exciting for me; now I just watch.

A few questions. What is the relationship between asking "What am I?" and the flow of thoughts, perceptions, etc.? For example, do you address the question to particular thoughts, pains in the knee when sitting, etc.? When a thought comes, do you ask whom this thought is coming to? Do you do it with each thought as it comes in turn? each dominant sensation? or do you simply keep the question alive and let everything else come and go? In other words, are you mindful of the thought content and ask the question with each particular event in mind, or do you not pay much attention to the content of the mind, pouring energy into the question instead? Related to this are common student problems. Many students have asked how to work with problems like fear, anger, masturbation, etc. Should they enter into the content of the fear, anger, etc.? Should they acknowledge the fear and then ask to whom the fear is coming? Should they let it all happen and pour energy into the big question? Part of the problem seems to be that people can ask the question amidst the flow of ordinary thoughts, but when very dramatic states, personal problems come up, they find it hard to pay attention to the question, which seems remote.

I look forward to seeing you soon. When do you leave for California? I hope to be back in time for the August *sesshin.* It sounds like I won't recognize the Center—many changes.

Until then, I hope your English and health are good.

Love,
Byon Jo

P.S. Perhaps the most important lesson for me here is a negative one. Being exposed to so many different teachers and teachings has only made your approach stand out with even greater clarity. People here read, talk, and think even more than I do!!!! Can you believe that??

August 15, 1974

How are you, Byon Jo?

Thank you for your long letter. I already understand that your teaching is very good. Before, you only understood everything; now you have attained the HIT.

Drinking, sex, drugs—these actions are neither good nor bad. But people get attached to these actions very easily. Young people in America are especially attached to sex. Zen Master Won Hyo says that being involved with sex is like

64

a porcupine who crawls into a rat's hole: easy to go in, but impossible to back out, no matter how hard he tries. People make new karma through their attachment-actions. Karma means hindrance. Hindrance is suffering. If someone is not attached to drinking, sex, etc., then there is no hindrance. No hindrance is freedom. Freedom means Big I. You must check to find out if these people are attached to drink and sex. Many people think, "I am not attached to such-and-such." But "I am not attached" is attachment-thinking. "I am not attached" is the same as "I am attached."

About "What am I?"—The true "What am I?" is the complete question. Only don't-know mind. All the questions which you asked me in your letter are thinking. If you keep the complete "What am I?", then you don't know "What am I?" All thinking has been cut off, so how can the question appear? Asking who is thinking is not the correct way. This is opposites thinking. This is an opposites question, not the complete question, the perfect question. Pain is pain, the question is the question. Why ask the question about pain? If you are keeping the complete question, there is no pain. These actions—anger, fear, etc.—are made by past karma, so the result is actions done in anger, etc. If a person sits Zen, he will make his karma disappear and he will no longer be caught up in these actions. So when you are angry, afraid, etc., only try Zen. If you happen to get angry, that's all right, don't worry. "I want to cut off anger!"—this is thinking. Anger is not bad, not good. Only don't be attached to it. Only ask "What am I?" and the action will soon disappear.

When the Buddha was alive, there was a prostitute called Pass-a-million. Every day she sold her body many times. Every day many different men came and had sex with her. But any man who had sex with her would become enlightened. So she was only using sex to teach Buddhism. When a man came to her, he had many desires. But after being with her, he had no desires, he understood his true self, and he went away with a clear mind. This sex is saving-all-people sex. But if I have sex just because I like it, because of my own desires, it will result in suffering. So actions themselves are not good and not bad; only the intention is important. If you think something is good, it is good; if you think it is bad, it is bad. If you want to cut off all thinking and all karma, you must practice Zen.

Me, too, I miss you. When will you come back to the Cambridge Zen Center? I will leave for California on Sept. 17 or 18. I will be in Cambridge during the August *sesshin* with you.

Here is a question for you: Whenever anyone asked Zen Master Lin-chi a question, he would shout "KATZ!!!" Zen Master Dok Sahn would only hit the questioner. Zen Master Ku-ji would only lift up one finger. Are these three answers the same or different? If you answer me, I will hit you thirty times. And if you don't answer, I will hit you thirty times. What can you do?

See you soon.
S.S.

29. Practicing Zen

One day, after a Dharma talk at the Vihara in Washington, D.C., a student asked Seung Sahn Soen-sa, "How should I practice Zen?"

Soen-sa said, "Don't you know?"

The student said, "I believe that the name and form of all things are different, but that their substance is the same. So to practice Zen I have to become one with the universe."

Soen-sa said, "What is this 'one'?"

"Everything."

"Once, when Zen Master Dong Sahn was asked, 'What is Buddha?', he said, 'Three pounds of flax.' What does this mean?"

"Three pounds of flax."

"Very good! But you are holding a stick and trying to hit the moon."

"That is Buddha-nature."

Soen-sa said, "Your head is a dragon, but your tail is a snake."

The student became confused and couldn't answer.

Soen-sa said, "I don't give acupuncture to a dead cow."

"Mooooo."

Soen-sa said, "The arrow has already passed downtown."

The student again was silent.

Soen-sa said, "Dong Sahn said that Buddha was three pounds of flax. In answer to the same question, Zen Master Un-mun said, 'Dry shit on a stick.' Are these two answers the same or different?"

"*You* tell *me*."

"I don't know. Ask my student."

He asked the student, who answered by shouting "KATZ!!!"

Soen-sa said, "Do you understand?"

The first student shouted "KATZ!!!"

Soen-sa said, "Very good. But your understanding is still only conceptual. Sometimes your answers are 'like this,' sometimes they show an attachment to emptiness. I will explain the Zen circle once more. At 90° the book is the pencil, the pencil is the book. At 180° you can only answer with a hit or a shout. At 270° the pencil is angry, the book laughs. At 360° the book is blue, the pencil is yellow. Now which one of these four answers is the best?"

The student said, "They're all good."

Soen-sa hit him and said, "Today is Saturday."

30. It Is Your Mind That Is Moving

November 24, 1974

Dear Soen-sa-nim,

Do you remember me? Here is a picture of myself.

I have some questions:

In the fall, there are leaves on the ground. If they are on a person's lawn, he comes out of his house and sweeps them together into little piles. In the afternoon, the wind comes and blows all the leaves away. Most people are very mad at the wind. Some of them go out again and sweep the new leaves into new piles. But again, the wind comes and blows them away. The wind always blows all the dead leaves away. Then what work must be done? Should a person always sweep leaves into piles and feel bad because he knows the wind will come soon?

If the tree has no roots, then how can it stand?

I hope to see you next summer. I look forward to that time very much. See you then.

Peter

November 29, 1974

Dear Peter,

Thank you for your letter. If a person goes outside and stays with leaves and wind and people, he cannot find his way back home. Why are you attached to leaves and wind and people's anger? Who is it that sees these leaves? Who?

Long ago in China, the Sixth Patriarch once passed two monks who were arguing about a flag blowing in the wind. One monk said, "It is the flag that is moving." The second monk said, "It is the wind that is moving." The Sixth Patriarch said, "You are both wrong. It is not the flag, it is not the wind: it is your mind that is moving." In the same way, with the leaves, wind, anger, etc., when your mind is moving, then actions appear. But when your mind is not moving, the truth is just like this. The falling of the leaves is the truth. The sweeping is the truth. The wind's blowing them away is the truth. The people's anger also is the truth. If your mind is moving, you can't understand the truth. You must first understand that form is emptiness, emptiness is form. Next, no form, no emptiness. Then you will understand that form is form, emptiness is emptiness. Then all these actions are the truth. And then you will find your true home. If you find your true home, come to me any time and tell me. I will check whether you have found it or not.

You say, "If the tree has no roots, how can it stand?" I say, "The dog runs after the bone." You must not be attached to words. First attain true emptiness. If you do not dwell in emptiness, you will get freedom and no hindrance. Then you will understand that the tree has no roots. Thinking is no good. Put it all down. Only "What am I?" This don't-know mind is very important. If you keep it for a long time, you will understand this tree without roots.

I will try to send you the newsletters. See you soon.

S.S.

31. Bodhisattva Attachment

One evening, after a Dharma talk at the Boston Dharmadhatu, a student asked Seung Sahn Soen-sa, "Is the Bodhisattva attached to compassion?"

Soen-sa said, "The universe is infinite; all people are infinite. So the Bodhisattva's attachment is infinite. A Bodhisattva attachment is no attachment. No attachment is a Bodhisattva attachment."

The student said, "Does he have it in mind to save all people or does this just happen wherever he is?"

Soen-sa said, "Do you understand what the Bodhisattva is?"

"No."

"First, understand what the Bodhisattva is. Then you will understand the Bodhisattva's attachment. The Bodhisattva is your true self. Your true self is Big I. Big I is all people. All people and I become one mind. So Bodhisattva action is always for all people. When people are happy, the Bodhisattva is happy. When people are sad, the Bodhisattva is sad. He always acts together with all people."

The student bowed and said, "Thank you."

32. Five Kinds of Zen

One Sunday night, after a Dharma talk at the Providence Zen Center, a student asked Seung Sahn Soen-sa, "How many kinds of Zen are there?"

Soen-sa said, "Five."

"What are they?"

"They are: Outer Path Zen, Common People's Zen, Hinayana Zen, Mahayana Zen, and Utmost Vehicle Zen."

"Could you explain each of these?"

Soen-sa said, "Zen is meditation. Outer Path Zen includes many different types of meditation. For example, Christian meditation, Divine Light, Transcendental Meditation, etc.

"Common People's Zen is concentration meditation, Dharma Play meditation, sports, the tea ceremony, ritual ceremonies, etc.

"Hinayana meditation is insight into impermanence, impurity, and non-self.

"Mahayana meditation is: 1) insight into the existence and nonexistence of the nature of the dharmas; 2) insight into the fact that there are no external, tangible characteristics, and that all is emptiness; 3) insight into existence, emptiness, and the Middle Way; 4) insight into the true aspect of all phenomena; 5) insight into the mutual interpenetration of all phenomena; 6) insight that sees that phenomena themselves are the Absolute.

"These six are equal to the following statement from the Avatamsaka Sutra: 'If you wish to thoroughly understand all the Buddhas of the past, present, and future, then you should view the nature of the whole universe as being created by the mind alone.'

"Finally, there is Utmost Vehicle Zen, which is divided into three types: Theoretical Zen, Tathagata Zen, and Patriarchal Zen."

The student then asked, "Which of the five kinds of Zen is the best?"

Soen-sa said, "Do you understand your mind?"

"No."

"When you don't understand your mind, all Zen is no good. When you understand your mind, all Zen is best."

"I want to understand my mind. What kind of Zen is the best training?"

Soen-sa said, "Understanding one's mind is the aim of Utmost Vehicle Zen."

"You mentioned before that this Zen is further divided into three kinds. Which of the three is the best training?"

Soen-sa said, "The three kinds are only one, not three. Intellectual understanding of Zen is Theoretical Zen. The attainment of emptiness, the unity of mind and the universe is Tathagata Zen. 'Like this' is Patriarchal Zen. This means a relaxed mind, the attainment of Big I. Big I is infinite time and infinite space."

The student said, "That's all very difficult. I don't understand."

Soen-sa said, "I will explain to you. The Heart Sutra says, 'Form is emptiness, emptiness is form.' So your substance and the substance of all things is the same. Your original mind is Buddha, Buddha is your original mind."

Then, holding a pencil in his hand, he said, "This is a pencil. Are you and the pencil the same or different?"

"The same."

Soen-sa said, "That's right. This is Theoretical Zen."

"What is Tathagata Zen?"

"The Mahaparinirvana Sutra says, 'All formations are impermanent; this is the law of appearing and disappearing. When appearing and disappearing disappear, then this stillness is bliss.' This means that when there is no appearance or disappearance in your mind, that mind is bliss. This is a mind devoid of all thinking. So I ask you again: Are this pencil and you the same or different?"

The student said, "The same."

Soen-sa said, "If you say 'the same,' I will hit you thirty times. If you say 'different,' I will still hit you thirty times. What can you do?"

The student couldn't answer and became very confused.

Soen-sa hit the floor and said, "If you keep your mind as it is just now, this is Tathagata Zen. Do you understand?"

"I don't know."

"This don't-know mind has no Buddha, no Dharma, no good, no bad, no light, no dark, no sky, no ground, no same, no different, no emptiness, no form, no anything in it. This is a truly empty mind. Empty mind is the mind which does not appear or disappear. Keeping this mind at all times is Tathagata Zen. Before, you said that the pencil and you are the same. This 'same' is thinking, so I said I would hit you thirty times. Do you understand?"

The student said, "A little."

"A little understanding is good. But if you ask me, 'Are the pencil and you the same or different,' I will hit the floor. When you understand why I hit the floor, you will understand Tathagata Zen."

"Thank you. Would you now explain Patriarchal Zen?"

Soen-sa said, "A person once asked Zen Master Mang Gong, 'What is Buddhism?' Mang Gong said, 'The sky is high, the ground is wide.' Do you understand what this means?"

"I don't know."

Soen-sa said, "That's right. 'Like this' is enlightenment. Patriarchal Zen is enlightenment Zen. An eminent teacher said:

1. 'Sky is ground, ground is sky: sky and ground are constantly changing.
   'Water is mountain, mountain is water: water and mountain are emptiness.
2. 'Sky is sky, ground is ground: how can they ever change?

'Mountain is mountain, water is water: the truth is just like this.'

"The first verse above is Tathagata Zen, and the second is Patriarchal Zen.

"A man once asked Zen Master Dong Sahn, 'What is Buddha?' He said, 'Three pounds of flax.' The man didn't understand, so he went to another Zen Master, described his encounter with Dong Sahn, and asked, 'What does "three pounds of flax" mean?' The Zen Master said, 'In the North, pine; in the South, bamboo.' The man still didn't understand, so he went to one of his friends who had been practicing Zen for some time. His friend said, 'You open your mouth, your teeth are yellow. Do you understand?' 'I don't know.' 'First understand your mind, then all of this will be clear.' "

Then Soen-sa asked the student, "Do you understand?"

The student said, "Yes. Thank you."

"What do you understand?"

" 'Like this' is Patriarchal Zen."

Soen-sa asked "What is 'like this'?"

The student couldn't answer. Soen-sa pinched his arm hard. The student yelled, "Owwwwwwwwww!"

"This is 'like this.' What is in pain?"

"I don't know."

"You must understand what is in pain. Then you will understand Utmost Vehicle Zen, and see that everything in the universe is the truth."

33. The Color of Snow

One winter afternoon, during Yong Maeng Jong Jin at the Providence Zen Center, Seung Sahn Soen-sa went for a walk with some of his students. It had snowed the day before. Soen-sa asked one student, "What color is this snow?"

The student said, "White."

Soen-sa said, "You have an attachment to color."

The student clapped his hands.

Soen-sa said, "Your head is a dragon, but your tail is a snake."

He then asked another student, "What color is this snow?"

The student said, "You already understand."

Soen-sa said, "Then tell me."

The student said, "It's white."

Soen-sa said, "Is this the truth?"

The student said, "Aren't you hungry?"

Soen-sa said, "Soon it will be time for lunch."

Another student said, "Go drink tea."

Soen-sa said, "I've already had some."

The student hit Soen-sa.

Soen-sa cried out, "Aie! Aie!"

34. Don't-Know Mind, Continued

One Thursday evening, after a Dharma talk at the Cambridge Zen Center, a student asked Seung Sahn Soen-sa, "If when you're driving you're just driving, when you sit Zen and ask 'What am I?' are you just the question?"

Soen-sa said, "Just the question. The *name* we give to clear mind is don't-know mind. So you must understand don't-know. Don't-know is don't-know. This is very important."

"But if I understand, then I don't have a don't-know mind, do I?"

"*Who* doesn't know?" (Laughter from the audience.) "When you keep don't-know mind—this is don't-know. You *are* don't-know. All people are given names, like Georgie, Roger, Stephen. But when you were born, you had no name. So mind is no mind. What is mind? I don't know. Your mind's name is don't-know."

"When you're driving, is your mind don't-know or are you just driving?"

"Only driving *is* don't-know." (Laughter.) "Only keep don't-know mind. Don't-know, okay?" (Laughter.)

"*What* don't you know?" (Laughter.) "I mean, if you're just driving, there's no knowing or not-knowing."

"When you are driving, do you have mind?"

The student was silent.

Soen-sa said, "Now your mind is don't-know mind. If

you are not attached to don't-know, there is only don't-know."

"Don't-know what?"

"What color is this door?"

"Brown."

"You say brown. This is don't-know. Do you understand?"

"I don't know." (Laughter.)

"Yah, you understand don't-know." (Laughter.)

"Are you attached to don't-know?"

"*You* are attached to don't-know! Attachment to words is no good. Only don't-know. When I drink water, I just drink water, I don't know, okay? So don't-know can drink water. Do you understand?"

"Why not say just that you're drinking water?"

"Now you are speaking. *Who* is speaking?"

The student was silent.

"Don't know. This don't-know is speaking."

"But if I'm just speaking, you don't need to say don't-know."

"Originally there is no name and no form. Its name is don't-know."

"Some Zen Masters say you must keep great doubt, which is don't-know mind, I guess. But they say there must come a point where you break through the great doubt into great enlightenment."

"Great doubt is don't-know. The names are different—great doubt, great question, great don't-know. There are many many names. My given name is Duk In, my monk's name is Haeng Won, my enlightenment name is Seung Sahn. I have many names. But none is my true name. When I was born, I had no name. The true name is no name. So great doubt, great question, don't-know—they are all the same."

"But when you are a baby, if your mother asks, 'What are you?', you don't answer, 'I don't know.' "

"Go ask a baby." (Laughter.)

"A baby doesn't think 'know' or 'don't-know'—it just is."

"Yah, it just is. Only don't-know. The baby is not attached to the question. You are attached to the question.

Don't-know is clear mind. Don't-know is before thinking. Don't-know is like this. Ask me now, 'What is don't-know?' "

"What is don't-know?"

Soen-sa picked up a cup of water and drank. "Do you understand? This is don't-know."

"But why say don't-know? If you're thirsty, you just drink. Why does a Zen person go around thinking 'I don't know'?" (Laughter.)

"If you are thinking, this is not don't-know." (Laughter.) "Don't-know is not-thinking. There is only don't-know. Socrates used to go around Athens saying, 'You must know yourself.' Once a student of his asked him, 'Do *you* know yourself?' Socrates said, 'I don't know, but I understand this don't-know.' I don't know, but when I am thirsty I drink. I don't know, but when I am tired I rest. Only this."

"The original question is 'What am I?' and your answer is 'I don't know.' *Who* doesn't know? You're still stuck in the question. You're on one end of it. Either I know or I don't know, and they're opposites. What if you throw the whole thing away and just live?" (Laughter.)

Soen-sa laughed and said, "You are thinking, thinking, thinking. So I will hit you thirty times!" (Laughter.) "What are you?"

The student was silent.

Soen-sa said, "You don't know. *This* mind. If you keep this mind, and are not attached to the words 'don't-know,' you will soon understand."

35. Zen and Tantra

One evening, after a Dharma talk at the Boston Dharma-dhatu, a student said to Seung Sahn Soen-sa, "At a recent seminar on Zen and Tantra, Chögyam Trungpa Rinpoche compared Zen to black and white and tantra to color. What do you think of this?"

Soen-sa smiled and said, "Which one do you prefer?" (Laughter from the audience.)

The student shrugged his shoulders.

Soen-sa said, "What color is your shirt?"

"Red."

"You are attached to color."

The student hesitated for a few moments, then said, "Maybe *you* are attached to black and white."

Soen-sa said, "The arrow has already passed downtown." There was a long silence. "Do you understand?" (A few giggles.) "Okay, I will explain: The dog runs after the bone." There was another long nervous silence. "Okay, I will explain even more." (Loud laughter.) "When you are thinking, your mind and my mind are different. When you are not thinking, your mind and my mind are the same. Now tell me —when you are not thinking, is there color? Is there black and white? Not thinking, your mind is empty mind. Empty minds means cutting off all speech and words. Is there color then?"

"I don't know."

"You don't know? I hit you! Now do you understand?" (Laughter.) "In original mind there is no color, no black and white, no words, no Buddha, no Zen, no Tibetan Buddhism."

The student bowed and said, "Thank you."

Soen-sa said, " 'Thank you?' What do you mean by 'Thank you'?"

"Only 'Thank you.' "

Soen-sa laughed and said, "Only 'Thank you' is good. I hope that you soon understand your true self."

The student said, "I've begun."

36. The 10,000 Questions Are One Question

April 12, 1974

Dear Soen-sa-nim,

Here are some questions for you:

How do you teach the Dharma? What do you teach? If you don't understand, what can you say about what Zen is?

Does a person learn things? Does a person understand more?

I hope you are enjoying sunny California—only cold rain in Providence, but we have money now for our new house.

See you soon,
Louise

April 20, 1974

Dear Louise,

How are you? Thank you for your beautiful postcard.
How are Alban, Roger, Bobby, Stephen, George, Suzie, and
Nick?

In your letter there are many questions. If you have questions, all things are questions. Why do you live? Why do you
die? How can you see, smell, and taste? Why does the sun
rise in the East? Why does the moon shine only at night?
Why does the earth revolve around the sun? And so on and
so forth.

But the ten thousand questions are only one question.
The one question is, "What am I?"

In the picture you sent me, someone is holding a sword.
This is a King's Diamond Sword. If you cut off all thinking
with it, the ten thousand questions disappear. Then tell me:
what is this Diamond Sword? If you can find it, your life is
absolutely free and your actions will have no hindrance. If
you don't find it, the question-demon will kill you, and you
will fall into hell. So put it all down!

It is better to keep your mouth shut as spring passes.

Here is a *kong-an:* "When the bell is rung, you put on
your *kesha."* What does this mean?

Your eyes, ears, nose, tongue, body, and mind all deceive
you.

The true you is without the six senses. But the six senses
use you, so you ask ten thousand questions. You must return
to your true self. Then you will understand.

The butterfly alights on the flower and drinks its nectar.

Here is a poem for you:

> What is Buddha?
> "Three pounds of flax."
> "Dry shit on a stick."
> I don't understand these words.
> The infant is sucking on his toes.

See you soon.
S.S.

37. Buddha Is Grass Shoes

One morning after practice, four students were having breakfast with Seung Sahn Soen-sa at the Corner Coffee Shop on East Twenty-First Street in New York City. One student told about an experience which he had had with some followers of the Nichiren sect. "Their mantra, *Nam yoho renge kyo,* seemed to me a quite powerful practice. But when I asked them what it meant, they didn't know and said it wasn't important to know. Is this correct?"

Soen-sa said, "In practice of this kind, correct understanding is not necessary. It doesn't matter whether you know that this mantra is the name of the Lotus Sutra or that Kwanseum Bosal is the name of the Bodhisattva Avalokiteshvara."

Another student said, "I've heard that certain mantras have power inherent in them—that Sanskrit sounds, for example, have some link to the energy of the universe. Does it make a difference which mantra you use?"

Soen-sa said, "Three things are important: first, your reason for doing the mantra; second, strong faith that the mantra works; and third, constant practice."

"So you can chant Coca-Cola all day long and it will work?"

"If someone tells you that the words Coca-Cola have power in them and you really believe that, then Coca-Cola will work for you. There is a good story about this:

"Three hundred years ago in Korea, there was a monk named Sok Du, which means 'Rock Head.' He was a very stupid man. The sutras were much too difficult for him, so he decided to study Zen. But sitting Zen was also too difficult. So he only did working Zen, in the kitchen and in the monastery fields. Twice a month the Zen Master would give a Dharma Speech, which would always fill Sok Du with confusion. One day, after the Dharma Speech, he went to the Zen Master and said, 'Master, I'm tired of being so stupid. Isn't there some way I can understand?'

"The Master said, 'You must ask me a good question.'

"Sok Du scratched his head and thought for a few minutes. Then he said, 'Okay. You are always talking about Buddha. What is Buddha?'

"The Master answered, *Juk shim shi bul,*' which means 'Buddha is mind.' But Sok Du misunderstood, and thought that the Master had said, *Jip shin shi bul,*' which means 'Buddha is grass shoes.'

" 'What a difficult *kong-an*!' Sok Du thought, as he bowed to the Master and left. 'How can Buddha be grass shoes? How will I ever understand?'

"For the next three years, Sok Du puzzled over this great question as he did his working Zen. He never asked the Master to explain; he just kept the question in his mind at all times. Finally, one day three years later, he was carrying a large load of firewood down the hill to the monastery. His foot hit a rock, he lost his balance, the wood fell, and his grass shoes went flying into the air. When they landed on the ground, they were broken, and he had attained enlightenment.

"Sok Du was very happy and very excited, so he went running back to the Zen Master. 'Master, Master, now I understand what Buddha is!'

"The Master looked at him and said, 'Oh? Then what is Buddha?'

"Sok Du took off one grass shoe and hit the Master on the head.

"The Master said, 'Is this the truth?'

"Sok Du said, 'My shoes are all broken!'

"The Master burst out laughing, and Sok Du flushed with joy."

At this, Soen-sa and his students also burst out laughing. Then they returned to their fried eggs and toast.

38. Three Interviews

One Sunday morning, a student came into the interview room at the Providence Zen Center and bowed to Seung Sahn Soen-sa. Soen-sa said, "What have you brought here?"

The student shouted "KATZ!!!"

Soen-sa said, "No. Give me another answer."

The student again shouted "KATZ!!!"

Soen-sa said, "You only say KATZ. How much does your KATZ weigh?"

The student answered, "Nothing."

Soen-sa hit him thirty times and the student left.

Another student came in and bowed.

Soen-sa said, "Long ago a student came to Un-mun and asked, 'What is Buddha?' Un-mun said, 'Dry shit on a stick.' Is this answer right or wrong?"

The student said, "Wrong."

Soen-sa asked, "Why is it wrong? If a person came and asked you 'What is Buddha?', what would your answer be?"

The student said, "Dry shit on a stick."

Soen-sa said, "Oh, very good. Now one more question. Zen Master Dong Sahn said, 'Buddha is three pounds of flax.' Are this answer and the other answer the same or different?"

The student hit the floor.

Soen-sa said, "I don't believe you."

The student said, "Birds fly in the sky, fish swim in the water."

Soen-sa said, "This is scratching your left foot when your right foot itches."

The student bowed and left.

Another student came in.

Soen-sa rang a bell and asked him, "When you hear this sound, is it inside your mind or outside?"

The student picked up the bell and rang it.

Soen-sa said, "Long ago Zen Master Un-mun, when asked 'What is Buddha?', answered, 'Dry shit on a stick.' Zen Master Dong Sahn answered the same question by saying, 'Three pounds of flax.' Which answer is better?"

The student said, "They're both no good."

Soen-sa asked, "Why?"

The student said, "Dry shit on a stick is dry shit on a stick. Three pounds of flax is three pounds of flax."

"Not bad. Now I have one more question for you. A person comes to the Providence Zen Center smoking a cigarette, drops ashes on the Buddha and blows smoke in his face. If you are the Zen Master, what can you do?"

The student said, "I would clean the Buddha."

"Good, but this person has an attachment to emptiness. He believes that only he is holy. You understand that his action is wrong. How can you teach him?"

The student hesitated and said, "I don't know. I'm not a Zen Master."

Soen-sa said, "If you do hard training, you will soon attain enlightenment and become a Zen Master."

The student bowed and left.

39. When the Lights Go Off, What?

One evening, after a Dharma talk at Yale University, a student asked Seung Sahn Soen-sa, "If form is non-form and non-form is form, is Buddha-mind thinking and thinking Buddha-mind?"

Soen-sa said, "Yes."

There was a long silence. Some people in the audience began to giggle.

Then Soen-sa said, "You already understand Buddhism. So I ask you: Who made thinking? Who made Buddha?"

The student was silent for a moment, then said, "I'm already thinking."

Soen-sa said, "Where does thinking come from?"

"From questioning."

"Questioning? Then where does questioning come from?"

"It comes from Buddha-mind."

Soen-sa laughed and said, "Don't make Buddha. Okay?" (Laughter from the audience.) "You say Buddha. Then what is Buddha?"

The student walked over to the light switch and turned off the lights. Then he turned them on again.

Soen-sa said, "Oho! Very good! But I have one more question for you: If you turn off the lights, what? If you turn on the lights, what?"

"Turning off the lights is nature before thinking."

Soen-sa laughed and said, "I hit you thirty times." (Laughter.) "When the lights go off, what? When the lights go on, what?"

"The lights off are Buddha-nature. The lights on are thinking."

Soen-sa said, "Okay, one more question. Buddha said, 'All things have Buddha-nature.' But when somebody asked Jo-ju, 'Does a dog have Buddha-nature?', Jo-ju answered, 'No!' Which one is correct?"

"I don't know."

Soen-sa said, "You must understand this. Then you will understand Buddha-nature. You say Buddha, Buddha-mind, Buddha-nature. These are only names. What is true Buddha-nature? You must understand Jo-ju's answer. Why did he say, 'No'? Before, I asked you, 'When the lights go off, what? When the lights go on, what?' When the lights go off, it is dark. When the lights go on, it is bright. Only like this. It is very simple." (Laughter.)

40. Testing the Mind

One Thursday evening, after a Dharma talk at the Cambridge Zen Center, a student asked Seung Sahn Soen-sa, "How does a Zen Master test his students' minds?"

Soen-sa said, "What is mind?"

The student was silent for a few moments, then said, "I don't know."

Soen-sa said, "Okay, I will ask you a question. One day somebody asked Zen Master Ma-jo, 'What is Buddha?' Ma-jo said, 'Mind is Buddha, Buddha is mind.' Later, somebody else asked him the same question and he answered, 'No mind, no Buddha.' Which answer is correct?"

The student hit the floor.

Soen-sa said, "I don't believe you."

The student was silent.

Soen-sa said, "You understand One; but you don't understand Two."

The student was still silent.

Soen-sa said, "Your first answer was good. But then you began to think, which is no good. Hitting the floor is a good answer. There is no correct or incorrect, so you only hit the floor. But does this hit mean 'No mind, no Buddha' or 'Mind is Buddha, Buddha is mind'?

"I can't say."

"Why not? Both Ma-jo's answers—'Mind is Buddha, Buddha is mind' and 'No mind, no Buddha'—are wrong. They are very low-class answers. As soon as you say 'mind,' you create 'not-mind'; as soon as you say 'Buddha', you create 'not-Buddha.' So Zen Master Jo-ju said, 'Even mentioning Buddha is like dumping shit on your head.' Both 'mind' and 'Buddha' are opposites words. They are not the Absolute. So both Ma-jo's answers are very bad teaching."

"No."

"No? Why no?"

"Because he's right for the person asking the question."

"The true Buddha cannot be expressed in words. If you were a Zen Master and somebody asked you, 'What is Buddha?', what would you answer?"

The student was silent.

Soen-sa said, "Only silence? Then this person won't understand. Suppose this person is very wild and hits you. What will you do then? Will you just continue to sit in silence?"

"I'd hit him back."

"Then he says, 'Your head is a dragon, your tail is a snake.' When you just sat in silence, that was a very good answer. But when you hit the person back, that wasn't so good. His hit was only to test your mind. So he says, 'Your head—your first answer—is a dragon, but your tail—your next answer—is only a snake.' "

"A dragon is a dragon, a snake is a snake."

"Then he says, 'The dog runs after the bone.' "

"Then I bow."

"Then he says, 'You must do more hard training!' " (Laughter from the audience.) "This is how a Zen Master tests his students' minds." (Loud laughter.)

The student laughed and bowed to Soen-sa.

41. What Is Death?

One morning, during Yong Maeng Jong Jin at the Providence Zen Center, a student walked into the interview room and bowed to Seung Sahn Soen-sa.

Soen-sa said, "Do you have any questions?"

The student said, "Yes. What is death?"

Soen-sa said, "You are already dead."

The student said, "I'm only dying. I haven't really experienced death yet. I don't even understand what that would mean."

Soen-sa hit him.

The student became confused and couldn't answer.

After a few moments, Soen-sa said, "When you think death, you make death. When you think life, you make life. When you are not thinking, there is no life and no death. In empty mind, is there a you? Is there an I?"

"No."

"You say No. You must understand No. This No is no self, no other, no body, no mind, no world. So it is no life and no death. This is true emptiness. True emptiness is before thinking. Before thinking is just like this. So life is only life; death is only death. You must not be attached to names and forms. It is like a clear mirror. In a clear mirror, all is nothing; there is only the clear mirror. Red comes, the mirror is red. Yellow comes, there is yellow. A woman comes, there is a woman. A man comes, there is a man. Death comes, there is death. Life comes, there is life. But all of these do not exist. The mirror does not hold on to anything. There is only the coming and the going. This is before thinking: all things are just as they are. The name for this mind is original pure mind. You must find your original face. Then you will not make life or death."

The student bowed, and the interview continued.

The next morning, the same student walked into the interview room and bowed.

Soen-sa said, "Do you have any questions?"

"Yes. What is death?"

"You are already dead."

"Thank you very much. Now I understand."

Soen-sa said, "You understand? Then what is death?"

The student said, "You are already dead."

Soen-sa smiled and bowed.

42. Wanting Enlightenment

After a Sunday night Dharma talk at the Providence Zen Center, Seung Sahn Soen-sa said to his students, "If you throw away all thoughts of attainment, you will then come to see the real purpose of your quest. Some of you want to reach enlightenment and become Zen Masters as quickly as possible. But as long as you have a thought like this, you will never attain anything. Just cut off all thoughts and conceptions. Then, as you work hard on your *kong-an,* all your questions and doubts will come to form one great mass. This mass will grow and grow, until you don't care about eating or sleeping or anything but finding the answer to the great question. When you find yourself in this state, enlightenment will not be far away."

A student asked, "If we didn't want to get enlightened, why would we take the trouble to come here?"

Soen-sa said, "Desire and aspiration are two different things. The idea that you want to achieve something in Zen meditation is basically selfish. 'I want to get enlightened' means '*I* want to get enlightened.' But aspiration is not for myself, it is not a merely individual desire, it transcends the idea of self. It is desire without attachment. If enlightenment comes, good. If enlightenment does not come, good. Actually, this *is* enlightenment.

"Could you explain why?"

"Originally there is no enlightenment. If I attain enlightenment, it is not enlightenment. As the Heart Sutra says there is 'no-attainment, with nothing to attain.' Enlightenment is not enlightenment. It is just a teaching word."

"What does it teach?"

"When you are hungry, eat. When you are tired, rest."

"Sometimes I feel that meditating is itself very selfish. I really don't feel I'm going to help others by sitting Zen. . . ."

"What are you? What is this self that is feeling selfish? If you understand this, you will know that there is no real difference between your self and all beings in the universe. Ultimately, they are one and the same. You include all beings. So if you are coming here for your own sake, you are coming for the sake of all beings."

Another student said, "I don't understand the difference between desire and aspiration. If you have the idea 'I want to save all beings,' isn't there still the duality, I and all beings?"

Soen-sa said, "Before you use these words, you must understand what the self is."

"Okay, tell me, what is it?"

"Did you have dinner?"

"Yes."

"What did it taste like?"

"It tasted like rice."

"I will hit you thirty times."

"Ouch!"

The first student said, "What you taught before is as clear as day. But I still feel selfish when I come here and my children want me to be with them at home."

Soen-sa said, "Let me ask you this: If you could do anything your heart desired, what would you want to do most of all?"

"Get enlightened."

"And after you get enlightened, what will you do then?"

The student was silent for several moments. Then she said, "I don't know."

Soen-sa said, "You want most of all to attain enlightenment. And you don't have any idea what you will do with it. That not-knowing is your true self. As long as you cling to your desire to attain enlightenment, you will never attain. But desire brings you here to sit Zen. So come and sit. That is a first step."

43. The True Way for Women

One Thursday evening, after a Dharma talk at the Cambridge Zen Center, a young woman asked Seung Sahn Soen-sa, "What is the true way for women?"

Soen-sa said, "I don't know—I'm not a woman." (Laughter from the audience.) Then, after a few moments, "Okay, I ask you: what is woman?"

The student said, "I don't know."

Soen-sa said, "*This* is the true way. Only don't-know mind. In don't-know mind, there is no woman, no man, no old, no young, no people, no Buddhas, no self, no world, nothing at all. If you understand this don't-know mind, you understand the true way. If you don't understand don't-know mind, you cannot understand the true way. Okay?"

"I don't know."

"Then you must keep don't-know mind."

"But if things are only like this, then man is man and woman is woman!"

"Yes."

"So the true way for men and the true way for women —are they the same or different?" (Laughter.)

Soen-sa said, "Ah, that is a very big question!" (Laughter.) "So I ask you: man and woman—are they the same or different?"

"I asked you first!"

"Then you have already attained the true way for women." (Laughter.)

"I don't understand."

Soen-sa said, "Then I will hit you." (Laughter.) "Do you understand now?"

The student bowed.

44. Can You See Your Eyes?

One evening, after a Dharma talk at the Boston Dharma-dhatu, a student asked Seung Sahn Soen-sa, "What is the difference betwen *shikan taza*—'only sitting'— and *kong-an* practice?"

Soen-sa said, "When I was in Los Angeles last month, many people asked me about the difference between Soto and Rinzai Zen. I answered, 'They are the same.' Only the externals are different. Soto uses awareness of breathing to cut off thinking. *Kong-an* Zen uses the *kong-an* to cut off thinking. Only the method is different. Cutting off thinking and becoming clear mind is the same. They are two doors into the same room. If I am attached to *shikan taza* or to the *kong-an,* then they are different. But if I am not attached, then they are the same."

The student said, "Sometimes you hear of people struggling with *kong-ans* for years. That bothers me. The implication is that either they're on the wrong path or it takes all that time to realize you shouldn't struggle at all. Are you saying there shouldn't be a struggle?"

Soen-sa said, "Keeping the mind that desires enlightenment is the wrong way to use the *kong-an.* Only keep the great question. The great question means cutting off all thinking, becoming empty mind. So the mind that keeps the great question *is* enlightenment! You are already enlightened, but you don't know it. So after much hard training: ah, *this* is enlightenment! It is very easy. Can you see your eyes?"

"No."

"You have no eyes? You *have* eyes. Can you grasp your mind?"

"No."

"You have no mind? It is the same. Can you see this cup? Can you hear my voice?"

"Yes."

"This is your mind. My eyes can't see my eyes. To try to see my eyes is the wrong way. My mind can't understand my mind. So to try to understand my mind is the wrong way. If you cut off this mind, you will soon attain enlightenment. I can see this cup; so I have eyes. I can hear this sound; so I have mind. What am I? I am asking I. So there are no opposites. Having no opposites is the Absolute. So all thinking is cut off. Only don't know, only empty mind. This is my true self. It is very easy."

45. Special Medicine and Big Business

One spring afternoon, three students were having tea in Seung Sahn Soen-sa's room at the Providence Zen Center. One student said to Soen-sa, "Many people have come to Zen as a result of their experience with psychedelics, or 'special medicine,' as you call it. Is taking psychedelics good or bad?"

Soen-sa said, "The question of good or bad is not important. It is neither good nor bad. What is important is why they take this medicine. Do you understand?"

Another student said, "What do you mean by good and bad?"

Soen-sa said, "Taking the medicine in order to understand is good. Taking the medicine because of the good feelings it gives you is not so good."

"Then it's possible to come to an understanding through special medicine?"

"It is possible. Many people are attached to name and form. They take this medicine and for five or ten hours it is the same as death. They have no hindrance from their body and their body's desires. It is like a dream. There is only the free action of their consciousness, the free play of the Karma I. So they understand that all life is empty. Life is death; death is life. They understand very clearly that fighting and differences among people are unnecessary, are just the result of wrong thinking. They no longer desire to be rich or successful. Rich or poor, success or failure—it is all the same. It comes to the same thing when you are dead."

The first student said, "You've just convinced me to take special medicine twice a day!"

Soen-sa said, "Taking it once or twice can be very helpful. But taking it more often is dangerous. It is very easy to become attached to special medicine. You are already a Zen student. So you already understand that life is empty; you understand what the true way is. When your body is sick, it is sometimes necessary to take a strong drug. But when you are healthy, you don't take drugs. So this special medicine cures some sickness, but it creates other sicknesses. After you take it, you have many attachments. You don't feel like working. You don't want to make money. You only want to relax or work in the garden or listen to music or enjoy art."

"Not make money? Heaven forbid!"

"This is an attachment to natural-style or hippie-style living. It is no good for a Zen student. Many people take special medicine and understand themselves. But their understanding is only thinking. It is not attainment. True attainment of emptiness means that all thinking has been cut off. There are neither likes nor dislikes. Natural-style living is good. Plastic-style living is good. There are no attachments to anything."

The third student said, "Soen-sa-nim, many different people practice Zen. I practice Zen; businessmen and lawyers practice Zen. I have an attachment to natural-style; they have an attachment to big-business-style. You don't say to them that they must give up business and only practice Zen, and you don't say to me that I must give up natural-style and only practice Zen. It's just different karma, isn't it?"

Soen-sa said, "Your life is natural-style; that's good. Businessman-style living is also good. What is important is *why* you are living this way. If you desire money for yourself or if you desire natural-style for yourself—this is no good. If you cut off your desires, then business is not business. It is Bodhisattva business. Natural-style is not natural-style. It is Bodhisattva action. So you can use business or natural-style living to teach all people the true way."

"You can teach natural-style living?"

"Yes, teaching natural-style is very good, as long as you are not attached to it. Natural-style is very high-class Bodhisattva action."

"Why?"

"True hippies have no hindrance. If I have no money, that's okay. If I don't have a house or a bed, that's okay. I can sleep anywhere, I can eat any food. My whole life is freedom. I am free to do anything. Having no hindrance means not being attached to anything. So this hippie-mind is very good; it is a very high-class mind. But many young people are attached to hippie-style or natural-style living. This is no good. If you are attached, then hippie-style becomes a hindrance. You must cut off all thinking and all desires for yourself. Then you will soon attain enlightenment. The hippie-mind is only one hair's-breadth away from enlightenment. If a hippie could cut off his attachment to being a hippie, he would soon discover, 'Oh, *this* is enlightenment!' One of my first students in America had very long blond hair, which he wore in a pony-tail. One day I said to him, 'I think it would be good if you cut your hair.' He said, 'No no, I like my hair the way it is.' I said, 'If you are attached to your hair, you cannot attain enlightenment.' 'Is this true?' 'Yah, enlightenment is complete freedom. If you are attached to your hair, then your hair is a hindrance. If you have a hindrance, you cannot attain enlightenment.' 'Okay, then I will cut my hair.' 'Fine. Now you don't need to cut it.' So he learned that being a true hippie is having no attachments. Afterwards, he did hard training and soon understood."

The first student said, "Is it possible for a businessman to have no hindrance?"

Soen-sa said, "Only if he has no desire. If he is working and earning money in order to help other people, then Zen is business, business is Zen. They are not two. All jobs are the same. Most people don't understand this. They are only interested in making a lot of money or becoming successful. This is small I. But if I make money to help all people, then business is good business. It is Big Business!"

46. Miracles

July 26, 1975

Dear Soen-sa-nim,

Somebody at the New Haven Zen Center asked me the following questions: "If a Zen Master is capable of doing miracles, why doesn't he do them? He is supposed to be a great Bodhisattva: doesn't this mean curing both physical and mental diseases? Why doesn't Soen-sa-nim do as Jesus did—make the blind see, or touch a crazy person and make him sane? Wouldn't even such a showy miracle as walking on water make many people believe in Zen, so that they would begin to practice and eventually come to understand themselves? So why doesn't he do miracles only for all people?"

How should I answer such questions?

Yours sincerely,
Mu Gak

August 3, 1975

Dear Mu Gak,

Thank you for your letter.

Many people want miracles, and if they witness miracles they become very attached to them. But miracles are only a technique. They are not the true way. If a Zen Master used miracles often, people would become very attached to this technique of his, and they wouldn't learn the true way. If a doctor gave a sick person medicine that cured his sickness but gave him another sickness, would you call him a good doctor? It is true that people might be attracted to Zen if a Zen Master were to walk on water. But if they came for this reason, they would find actual Zen practice too difficult, or too boring, or too unmiraculous, and they would soon leave.

You know the story about Zen Master Huang Po. He was traveling with another monk, and they came to a river. Without breaking stride, the monk walked across the water, then beckoned to Huang Po to do the same. Huang Po said, "If I'd known he was that kind of fellow, I'd have broken his legs before he reached the water."

A keen-eyed Zen Master understands people's karma. The Buddha said, "Karma that you have made for yourself can only disappear if you want it to. No one can make you want it to disappear." He also said, "I have many kinds of good medicine, but I can't take it for you." The Buddha has already given instructions for someone who is blind or disabled. But most people want easy solutions. They want someone else to do their work for them.

It's like a mother teaching her child. If a mother does everything for the child, the child will come to depend on her. A good mother makes the child do things for itself. Then it will grow up strong and independent. There is now a man in Korea who has proclaimed himself as Christ. Many people believe in him. After he washes his face and his feet, they take the water and drink it as medicine. And indeed, their sicknesses are miraculously cured. But it is their minds that are curing their bodies. They believe in this man so completely that he can do miracles. If they didn't believe, he wouldn't be able to do miracles. In the same way, when a boy and girl are in love, the first time they kiss, their lips are filled with magical energy. This man can touch his followers and it is as if his fingers were flowing with electricity. There are many religious leaders like this in India.

But this is not good teaching. It keeps the disciples dependent on the leader. They cannot understand how their own minds are creating the miracles. And it becomes difficult for them to act for themselves. Magic alone can't make bad karma disappear; it is only a technique. Did Jesus solve anything by raising Lazarus from the grave? Lazarus still had the same karma as before, and he still had to die.

One of the Buddha's disciples, Mong Nyon, was a great miracle-worker. One day, as he was meditating, he saw that the Kapila kingdom would soon be destroyed by a war. He thought, "If I don't do something, a week from today, at 11 a.m., our whole country will be in ruins." So he went to the Buddha and said, "Lord, do you know that next week many of your people are going to be killed?"

"Yes."

"Then why don't you save them?"

"I can't."

"But you have special energy and can do miracles. Why can't you save them?"

The Buddha said, "It is impossible to make merited karma disappear."

But Mong Nyon didn't believe him. He got very angry, because he thought the Buddha wasn't being compassionate. So he went and shrunk the whole kingdom and put it into an eating bowl. Then he took the bowl to the highest heaven, where all is peace and serenity. There, in the middle of the palace in the middle of Do Sol heaven, he left the bowl for seven days. After the allotted time had passed, Mong Nyon breathed deeply and said to himself, "Ah, everything is okay now." So he took the bowl and brought it back to earth. But when he took off the cover and looked inside, he saw that the miniature country had been devastated by a miniature war.

Magic is only a technique. Some people know how to do card tricks. It looks as if they have done something magical, but it is really a trick. We don't see what is actually happening. What we call magic is the same. It is taking a person's consciousness and manipulating it. This can indeed be very powerful. There was once a Chinese general who was a great magician. During a civil war, he conjured up an enormous army of gods, and sent it flying through the air. The opposing army was terrified, and many soldiers were killed by this god-army. But the opposing general happened to be a wise man. He understood what was going on. So the next day he called his troops together before a large crystal ball which he had put up on a high post. "You must all gaze intently at this crystal," he said, "and keep your minds clear of all thinking. Then you will be safe. But if you look around or begin to think, you will certainly be killed by the gods." So all the soldiers kept their minds clear and couldn't be manipulated by magic. Soon the army of gods appeared. They hung in the air for a moment; then all that could be seen was a bunch of dry leaves floating down to the ground.

If someone wants to be able to do miracles, it is possible to learn how. But this is not the correct way. Keen-eyed Zen Masters seldom use magic or miracles, because these can't help people find the true way. The only way to make karma disappear is for your consciousness to become empty. Then there are no miracles. Then there are only correct views and correct practice. This is the true miracle.

Sincerely yours,
S. S.

47. A Dharma Speech

Given by Seung Sahn Soen-sa
at the San Francisco Zen Center
on February 9, 1975.

(Hitting the table with his Zen stick) Do you understand this? If you do, you understand One. If you don't, you separate things into ten thousand classes and one thousand levels.

(Hitting the table) Do you understand this? If you do, you understand the ten thousand classes and one thousand levels. If you don't, you have an attachment to One.

(Hitting the table) Do you understand this? If you open your mouth and say that you understand, I will hit you thirty times. And if you say that you don't understand, I will still hit you thirty times.

Why?

KATZ!!!

Spring air fills the universe, and flowers are blossoming everywhere.

If you proclaim this, you shut the mouths of all Buddhas and all eminent teachers. So how can you hear what they say? To hear what they say, you must understand what sitting Zen is.

When you are able to stay perfectly clear by cutting off all thinking and yet not falling into a trance-like sleep, this is sitting. When inside and outside become one, and no circumstances can hinder you, this is Zen.

When you understand sitting Zen, you understand yourself. In your mind there is a diamond sword. If you want to understand yourself, take it and cut off good and bad, long and short, coming and going, high and low, God and Buddha. Cut off all things.

You must proceed as if you were walking on thin ice, concentrating totally on each one of your steps. If you make one wrong move, you will die and go to hell like an arrow.

Passing beyond this realm of not-thinking, you reach the land of true emptiness. True emptiness is before thinking. This land is without words or speech; so there are no mountains, no rivers, no East, West, North, or South, no God, no Buddha.

But if you stay there, you will become attached to emptiness, and not even Buddha will be able to save you.

When you are hanging by your hands from a mountain ledge and can let go, not thinking of life or death, then you will have true freedom. You can see the wooden dog eating steel and shitting fire. You make friends with the hairy-shelled turtle and the rabbit with horns. You learn to play the flute which has no holes. But where does the sound of the flute come from?

Leave this place behind, and you understand that birds sing, hills are green, and the sky is blue. Seeing, hearing, smelling, tasting, touching—the truth is just like this. This is the language of Buddha and eminent teachers. The sounds of rivers and birds are the sutras; earth and sky are the very body of the Buddha.

(Holding up his Zen stick) Then do you see this?

(Hitting the table) Do you hear this?

This stick, this sound, and your mind—are they the same or different?

If you say they are the same, that is not permitted, and the stick will hit you. If you say they are different, that is not permitted, and the stick will hit you. If you say they are both different and the same, that too is not permitted, and the stick will hit you even harder.

Why?

KATZ!!!

If you don't enter the lion's den, you will never capture the lion.

48. A Little Thinking, A Little Sparring

One evening, after a Dharma talk at the Boston Dharma-dhatu, a student said to Seung Sahn Soen-sa, "They say that you reach a point in Zen meditation where there's a cessation of thought, or, alternatively, there's a cessation of the watcher, although thoughts continue. Could you comment on that?"

Soen-sa said, "Where does thinking come from?"

The student pointed to his forehead and said, "It's supposed to be here."

"Where does thinking go?"

"Ummm . . . I don't know."

"What is thinking?"

"Something that happens, I guess. An awareness."

Soen-sa said, "Thinking is a name which people make." Then, pointing to a piece of paper, "The name for this is paper. If you ask a cat what this is, the cat will not say it is a piece of paper. River, mountain, sun, moon—all are names. For a cat, the sun is not the sun; for a dog, the moon is not the moon. Go point to the moon and ask a dog, 'What is this?'" (Laughter from the audience.) "People's thinking makes all these things. So thinking is your mind. Mind is no mind. So thinking is no thinking."

The student said, "I sort of realize that. But how do you stop thinking?"

Soen-sa said, "Okay, I will teach you. Come here." The student came to the front of the room and sat down in front of Soen-sa. Soen-sa handed him a cup of water and said, "Drink this." The student drank. Soen-sa said, "Is it hot or cold?"

The student was silent for a few moments, then said, "It tastes good."

Soen-sa said, "This is thinking. When you drank the water, you were not thinking. When I asked you if it was hot or cold, you were thinking, 'What answer is good?' This is thinking. When you drank, you only drank." Then, holding up the piece of paper, "What is this?"

The student was silent.

"Why don't you answer?"

"Well, you want me to say it's a piece of paper." (Laughter.)

Soen-sa said, "Very late. Many thinking." (Laughter.) "Here, come closer." The student came closer. "Bend down." The student bent down, and Soen-sa hit him on the back. "What was that?"

"Well, it was a noise."

"When I hit you, you didn't know. Why did I hit you?"

"Umm, to shake me up a little?"

"Do you understand what my hit means?"

"It felt kind of nice."

"Feeling good is your action. Do you understand what *my* action means?"

"Maybe you're trying to teach me."

Soen-sa said, "Once Buddha was staying at Vulture Peak. Every day he would speak before many people. One day he came and sat before an audience of twelve hundred people. Everyone waited for him to begin, but he sat in silence. One minute passed, then two minutes, then three minutes. Only silence. Finally Buddha held up a flower. Nobody understood but Mahakashyapa. He saw the flower and smiled. Buddha said, 'I have transmitted the true Dharma to you.' Now I ask you: when Buddha held up the flower, what did this mean?"

"He only lifted up the flower. To show it was his own action."

"If you were there and saw him lift up the flower, what would you do?"

"I'd pick it."

Soen-sa exclaimed, "Ah ha ha!" (Laughter.) "*You* are Buddha, okay?"

The student said, "I'm not Buddha." (More laughter.)

Soen-sa said, "If you pick the flower, Buddha hits you. What can you do?"

"Hit him back."

"Then Buddha says, 'You understand One, but you don't understand Two.' What would you answer?"

"I don't understand three."

"Then Buddha says, 'I thought you were a keen-eyed lion, but now I see you are a blind dog.' "

The student was silent.

Soen-sa said, "Okay, I will explain. What Buddha says means, 'Your hit is very good. I am Buddha, you are Buddha! So you hit back. Buddha and you are the same. This is a high-class answer. So Buddha once more tests you. 'You understand One, you don't understand Two.' Your answer to this was no good, so Buddha says, 'I thought you were a keen-eyed lion, but now I see you are a blind dog.' "

The student said, "Well . . ." and then was silent. Everybody laughed.

Soen-sa said, "You must open your mind's eye. Okay?"

The student said, "Thank you."

Soen-sa said, "You're welcome."

49. No-Attainment Is Attainment

One Thursday evening, after a Dharma talk at the Cambridge Zen Center, a student asked Seung Sahn Soen-sa, "If, as the Heart Sutra says, there is no attainment with nothing to attain, why do we practice Zen?"

Soen-sa said, "Do you understand no-attainment?"

The student said, "I don't know."

Soen-sa said, "No-attainment is attainment. You must attain no-attainment. So what is attainment? What is there to attain?"

"Emptiness?"

"In true emptiness there is no name and no form. So there is no attainment. If you say, 'I have attained true emptiness,' you are wrong."

"Is there a false emptiness?"

"The universe is always true emptiness. Now you are living in a dream. Wake up! Then you will understand true emptiness."

"How can I wake up?"

"I hit you." (Laughter from the audience.) Soen-sa said, "It is very easy."

The student said, "What is this dream?"

Soen-sa said, "*This* is a dream."

"Do I look like I'm dreaming?"

Soen-sa said, "Yah. What is not a dream? Give me one sentence of not-dream words." Then, after a few moments, "All is a dream."

"Are you dreaming?"

"Yah!" (Loud laughter.) "You make the dream, so I am having it. It is a good dream. It is a Zen dream. A Zen-lecture dream." (Laughter.) "But how can you wake up? This is very important. Your whole past life is the same as a dream, isn't it? The future is the same as a dream. And this present moment is the same as a dream. So tell me—how can you wake up?"

The student said, "You put me in an impossible situation. How can I wake up if I'm asleep?"

Soen-sa said, "Okay, let me ask you—what is good?"

"Good is thinking."

"Who made good?"

"I did."

"Where does I come from?"

"I comes from I."

"You understand the word 'I,' but you don't understand the true I. Where does I come from?"

"From thinking."

"Thinking is also a word. Where does thinking come from?"

The student was silent for a long time, then said, very slowly, "I really don't know."

Soen-sa said, "Yes! This is the complete don't-know mind. There are no words and no speech—there is only don't-know. Only don't-know means that all thinking is cut off. Cutting off all thinking is true emptiness. This is how you begin to wake up."

The student bowed and said, "Thank you. I have another question now. In daily life, many people ask us for our opinions and judgments. 'Do you like this? Do you like that?' Should we avoid such conversations?"

Soen-sa said, "Why should you avoid them?"

"Because they make me feel like an individual, a separate entity. I begin to feel my ego more strongly."

Soen-sa said, "When you are walking, your hand moves back and forth. This is not-thinking action. So if you talk, don't be attached to talking. No-attachment thinking is not thinking. If you are attached to your thinking, this creates karma. If you are not attached, you don't create karma. Today my English teacher at the Harvard Summer School gave me some homework. Very difficult!" (Laughter.) "How can I do this homework? Don't know. Only this big question. I eat, but there is no taste, there is only the big homework question inside. On the way home in the bus there is only my homework, so I forget to get off at the right stop. If you keep this mind, seeing is the same as not seeing, hearing is the same as not hearing, working is the same as not working. This is no-attachment thinking. There is only the big question. Then talking is no-attachment action. So it is not talking. You use your eyes, but there are no eyes. You use your mouth, but there is no mouth. If you keep a clear mind, red is red, white is white. But you are not attached to red or to white. There is only red, only white. 'I like this' is only 'I like this.' 'I don't like this' is only 'I don't like this.' This mind is the same as a child's mind. So here there is no-attainment, with nothing to attain. This means that before thinking there are no words and no speech. If you keep don't-know mind, there is no-attainment, with nothing to attain. Attainment is a name. This is thinking mind. Attainment and no-attainment are opposites. Before thinking is the Absolute. There are no words, no speech. So there is nothing. If you open your mouth, you are wrong. Then what is attainment? Only KATZ!!! Only HIT."

The student said, "It's very difficult to keep the kong-an while I'm working. What can I do?"

Soen-sa said, "In the beginning it is difficult. It is the same as driving a car. When you are learning to drive and somebody walks in front of your car, you step on the brake hard. This is thinking action. But after you have driven a lot, you step on the brake automatically when you need to stop. This is reflex action, not-thinking action. When you begin kong-an practice, the don't-know mind and your work are separate, fighting. But after much practice, don't-know mind is work mind, work mind is don't-know mind. When you do our morning chanting, there is only chanting. If you are thinking, you will forget the words or make a mistake. With don't-know mind it is very easy to remember. So you must ask yourself the big question, 'What am I?' "

The student said, "I feel like I've already understood that *kong-an*, understood true emptiness. But then I forget. I'm back in the world of duality. Is what I've understood not true emptiness?"

Soen-sa said, "If you understand emptiness, this is not emptiness. It is only a word. You understand the word 'emptiness.' Have you ever tasted *kim-chee*, Korean pickled cabbage? It is very hot. When guests come to dinner here, I tell them that *kim-chee* is very hot. But they don't really know what this 'hot' means until they experience it for themselves. So I give them a piece of *kim-chee*. Ow!! Hot!!!" (Laughter.) "Other people understand that *kim-chee* is hot, but they haven't tasted it. Once they taste it, then they really understand what hot means. They have attained 'hot.' So understanding 'hot' is not the same as attaining 'hot.' Many young Americans understand one mind. But this is not true understanding; it is only thinking. So understanding emptiness and attaining emptiness are different. If you attain emptiness one time, you have attained it forever. You don't forget. You say you understand emptiness. Then what is emptiness?"

"This is emptiness."

"*You* say it is emptiness. *I* say it is not emptiness. You have a hand, a voice, a body. In emptiness there is no hand, no voice, no body. What is true emptiness? This is very important. In true emptiness there are no words. If you open your mouth, you are wrong. So . . . what color is this door?"

The student was silent.

Soen-sa said, "What color is this?"

The student said, "You have eyes."

Soen-sa said, "Eyes? These are not eyes. They are holes in my face." (Laughter.) "I ask you once again—what color is this door?"

The student was silent.

Soen-sa said, "It is brown."

"But if I'd said brown, you would've said I'm attached to color!"

Soen-sa said, "Brown is only brown." Then, pointing to a glass of water, "What is this?"

"Water."

"Yah. Water is water. This is not thinking. When you said 'water'—*this* mind. This mind is very important. It is a clear mirror. Red comes, the mirror is red. Yellow comes, the mirror is yellow. Water comes, there is water. A door comes, there is a door. If you are not thinking, your mind is the same as a mirror. It is only like this. So true emptiness is clear mind. In original clear mind there is no name and no form. Nothing appears or disappears. All things are just as they are. If you are thinking, you are in a dream. You must cut off all your thinking and wake up."

50. True Sitting Zen

December 15, 1974

Dear Soen-sa-nim,

Maezumi Roshi asked me to write to you and ask if it is all right for me to study with him.

Susan and I spent three days with him at *sesshin*. He is a very aware man. Full to the top and empty as the sky. He is using your *kong-ans*. Sitting is becoming stronger.

See you.
Byon Mon

All pervading
stone breathing
zafu sitting
children play
wind blows
what more
ahh . . .
legs hurt

December 20, 1974

Dear Byon Mon,

Thank you for your letter. It is very good that you are sitting with Maezumi Roshi. I like him also.

If you continue studying with him, you must be careful not to be attached to his words and not to be attached to sitting Zen. You must understand what true sitting is, what true Zen is. True sitting means to cut off all thinking and to keep not-moving mind. True Zen means to become clear. Beautiful words and hard sitting are important. But attachment to them is very dangerous. Then you will not be able to understand true sitting Zen.

Once Zen Master To An was visiting another temple. He wasn't wearing his Zen Master clothes, only the clothes of a wandering monk. He began a conversation with one of the monks at the temple, who did not recognize that he was a Zen Master. Soon the monk began to talk about his Master. "Every day he does one thousand prostrations. He eats only once a day. He hasn't left the temple for thirty years. He is always sitting Zen. He is the greatest Zen Master in all of China."

To An said, "Well well, he sounds like an extraordinary man. I can't do any of these things. I can't bow a thousand times a day; but my mind is never lazy. I can't eat only once a day; but I never desire food. I can't stay in a temple for more than a short time; but wherever I go I have no hindrance. I can't sit Zen for very long; but I never give rise to thinking."

The monk said, "I don't understand."

To An said, "Go ask your Master to explain."

The monk bowed and went into the temple. Soon the Zen Master came running out to To An and prostrated himself three times in front of him. "You are a great Zen Master," he said. "Please let me become your disciple. I have been very attached to hard training. But now that I have heard your kind words, my mind is clear."

To An laughed and said, "No no, I can't be your teacher. You are already a great Zen Master. All you need to do is to keep the mind you had when you were bowing to me. Already you are a free man. Before, you were bowing, sitting, and eating only for yourself. Now it is for all people."

At these words, the Zen Master began to weep with joy. He bowed again to To An and said, simply, "Thank you."

Byon Mon, what do you think about this?

You said in your letter that Maezumi Roshi is "full to the top and empty as the sky." What does this mean? If you understand true emptiness, then you understand these words. If you understand these words, then you have already attained enlightenment. But if you have not attained enlightenment, then you don't understand these words.

Your poem is very nice. But I don't like words. So please send me a poem before words.

Sincerely yours,
S. S.

51. Samadhi vs. Satori

One Thursday evening, after a Dharma talk at the Cambridge Zen Center, a student said to Seung Sahn Soen-sa, "I understand that *samadhi* is a state that takes quite a while to attain. However, *satori* is a sort of instant enlightenment. How do the two differ?"

Soen-sa said, "If you are thinking, *samadhi* and enlightenment are different. If you cut off thinking, *samadhi* and enlightenment are the same. But when we explain them, they are different. *Samadhi* is one mind. Enlightenment is only like this. One mind; like this—these are different. But they are the same. So when we do the mantra, there is only the mantra. *Om mani padme hum, om mani padme hum.* All thinking is cut off. When I look, there is only the mantra; when I hear, there is only the mantra. This is *samadhi.* So if someone asks me, 'What color is this wall?', I answer, '*Om mani padme hum.*' If someone asks me, 'What is this?'" (holding up his hand) "I answer, '*Om mani padme hum.*' But enlightenment is: 'What color is the wall?' 'White.' 'What is this?' 'A hand.' So *samadhi* is only one mind, not-moving mind."

"Then it's the same as *satori.*"

"It is not the same. Yah, it is the same and not the same."

"I understand."

"Then I ask you: Once, during Buddha's lifetime, a woman was sitting in *samadhi*—very deeply into *samadhi.* She didn't wake up, only *samadhi,* as if she were dead. The Bodhisattva Manjushri, who is a tenth-class Bodhisattva, the highest class, tried to wake her, but couldn't. Finally a first-class Bodhisattva appeared, walked around her three times, and hit her on the back. She woke up immediately. Why couldn't this great Bodhisattva bring her out of *samadhi,* while the low-class Bodhisattva could? If you understand this, you will have a true understanding of *samadhi* and enlightenment. Do you understand?"

The student was silent.

Soen-sa said, "You must understand this. There is another *kong-an* with the same meaning. An eminent teacher said, 'If I kill my parents, I can repent to Buddha. But if I kill all Buddhas and eminent teachers, to whom can I repent?'"

The student said, "Myself?"

Another student called out from the back of the room, "Go drink tea!"

Soen-sa said, "Who said that?"

The student raised her hand.

Soen-sa said, "Oh, very good! Wonderful! These two *kong-ans* are the same *kong-an.* If you understand this, you understand *samadhi* and enlightenment."

52. Lin-Chi's KATZ

Whenever Zen Master Dok Sahn was asked a question, he would answer only by hitting the questioner. Zen Master Ku-ji would answer only by raising one finger, and Zen Master Lin-chi only by shouting "KATZ!!!" And so the stick of Dok Sahn, the finger of Ku-ji, and the KATZ of Lin-chi became famous.

Lin-chi always shouted "KATZ!!!" Sometimes the KATZ cut off people's thinking, sometimes it was a testing of Zen progress, and sometimes it opened up minds.

One day a person came and asked Lin-chi, "What is Buddhism?"

Lin-chi shouted "KATZ!!!" The person bowed and left.

Another day a person came and bowed. As soon as he raised his head, he shouted "KATZ!!!" Lin-chi made no reply, but as the person turned his head to leave, Lin-chi shouted "KATZ!!!"

Another person came and, as he was bowing, Lin-chi shouted "KATZ!!!" The person raised his head, looked at Lin-chi, and then shouted "KATZ!!!" Quickly Lin-chi shouted "KATZ!!!" and walked away.

Another person asked Lin-chi, "Nowadays, what are you doing?"

Lin-chi shouted "KATZ!!!"

These are Lin-chi's four ways of using KATZ. He used it freely and opened many students' minds.

One day a person asked Lin-chi, "What is Zen?" Lin-chi held up his horse-hair whip. The person shouted "KATZ!!!" Lin-chi hit him.

Again the person asked, "What is Zen?"

Lin-chi again held up the whip.

The person shouted "KATZ!!!"

Lin-chi immediately shouted "KATZ!!!"

The person was confused and didn't know how to answer. Lin-chi hit him.

One day many people gathered in the Zen room. Lin-chi was sitting on a high platform and said, "Inside a wall of pink flesh lives the Utmost Master. All day long this Master goes in and out through the six doors. Do you understand?"

One monk stood up and asked, "What is this Utmost Master?"

Lin-chi got up, ran down the steps, grabbed the monk, and shouted, "Tell me! Tell me!"

The monk hesitated. Lin-chi flung him away and said, "This Utmost Master is a lump of shit."

53. Nirvana and Anuttara Samyak Sambodhi

One Sunday morning, at the Providence Zen Center, a student walked into the interview room and bowed to Seung Sahn Soen-sa. Soen-sa said, "What is Nirvana?"

The student hit the floor.

"In the Heart Sutra, it speaks first of Nirvana, then of Anuttara Samyak Sambodhi. What is this?"

Again the student hit the floor.

"Then are the two the same?"

Again the student hit the floor.

"You only hit the floor. You are clinging to this answer. Give me another one."

The student hit the floor.

"You do not distinguish between red and white. You have eyes, but you are blind. A second offense is not permitted."

After the student had bowed and left, another student came in. Soen-sa said, "What is Nirvana?"

The student hit the floor.

"What is Anuttara Samyak Sambodhi?"

"When the sun comes up, the whole world is bright."

"Then are the two different?"

The student hit the floor.

"Is this the truth?"

"No."

"Then what is the truth?"

"Sunlight falls on the floor, and the cat lies sleeping."

Soen-sa said, "I will meet you again in five hundred years."

The student bowed and left.

54. Zen and the Arts

One day a student came to tea at the Providence Zen Center and asked Seung Sahn Soen-sa about the relationship between Zen and the arts.

Soen-sa said, "Zen is understanding life and death. Why are you alive?"

The student said, "I don't know."

Soen-sa said, "Why will you have to die?"

The student shrugged his shoulders.

Soen-sa said, "People live and die on the earth without understanding what life and death are. When you were born, you were only born. You didn't say, as you were coming out of your mother's womb, 'Now I am going into the world. Help me.' You just came, without wanting to be born or knowing why you were born. It is the same with death. When you die, you only die. You are not free to choose.

"Zen is the Great Work of life and death. Descartes said, 'I think, therefore I am.' I think, therefore I have life and death; I do not think, therefore I do not have life and death. So life and death are created by our own thinking. They exist because we think them into existence, and they cease to exist when we cease to think.

"If you are thinking, your mind, my mind, and all people's minds are different. If you are not thinking, your mind, my mind, and all people's minds are the same. . . ."

The student interrupted and said, "They're not different and not the same. These words are only thinking."

Soen-sa said, "Yes. If you cut off all thinking, this mind is before thinking. If you keep the before-thinking mind and I keep the before-thinking mind, we become one mind. Okay?"

The student said, "If we cut off all thinking, there's *no* mind."

Soen-sa laughed and said, "Very good. There is no mind. But its *name* is One Mind. Before thinking, there are no words or speech, no life or death. Then what is your true self?"

The student was silent.

Soen-sa said, "Zen is understanding your true self. You must ask yourself, 'What am I?' You must keep this great question and cut off all your thinking. When you understand the great question, you will understand yourself.

"Socrates used to walk around Athens telling his students, 'You must know yourselves.' Someone once asked him. 'Do *you* know yourself?' Socrates said, 'No. But I understand this not-knowing.' Zen is the same. It is not-knowing, not-thinking. 'What am I?' This is your true self.

"When you understand yourself, it is very easy to paint or write poems or do calligraphy or tea-ceremony or karate. You paint effortlessly; you write effortlessly. Why? When you are painting or writing or doing any action, you become totally absorbed in that action. You are *only* painting; you are *only* writing. No thinking gets between you and the action. There is only not-thinking action. This is freedom.

"If you are thinking, your mind wanders away from your action, and the flow of your painting or writing will be blocked, your tea-ceremony will be stiff or clumsy. If you are not thinking, you are one with your action. You are the tea that you're drinking. You are the brush that you're painting with. Not-thinking is before thinking. You are the whole universe; the universe is you. This is Zen mind, absolute mind. It is beyond space and time, beyond the dualities of self and other, good and bad, life and death. The truth is just like this. So when a Zen person is painting, the whole universe is present in the tip of his brush.

"There was once a great Japanese poet named Basho. He was a very bright young man, and as a serious Buddhist he had studied many sutras. He thought that he understood Buddhism. One day he paid a visit to Zen Master Takuan. They talked for a long time. The Master would say something and Basho would respond at length, quoting from the most profound and difficult sutras. Finally, the Master said, 'You are a great Buddhist, a great man. You understand everything. But in all the time we have been talking, you have only used the words of the Buddha or of eminent teachers. I do not want to hear other people's words. I want to hear your own words, the words of your true self. Quickly now—give me one sentence of your own.'

"Basho was speechless. His mind raced. 'What can I say? My own words—what can they be?' One minute passed, then two, then ten. Then the Master said, 'I thought you understood Buddhism. Why can't you answer me?' Basho's face turned red. His mind stopped short. It could not move left or right, forward or back. It was up against an impenetrable wall. Then, only vast emptiness.

"Suddenly there was a sound in the monastery garden. Basho turned to the master and said,

'Still pond—
a frog jumps in—
the splash.'

The Master laughed out loud and said, 'Well now! *These* are the words of your true self!' Basho laughed too. He had attained enlightenment.

"Later on, Basho went to Matsushima, one of the most beautiful places in Japan, where a poetry contest was being held. Poets from all over the country were there. Everyone wrote in praise of the loveliness of the countryside, the majestic snow-capped peak of Mount Fuji, the brilliant mirror surface of the lake, the sailboats flying across the water like great white birds, etc., etc. Basho wrote only three lines:

> Matsushima—
> ah Matsushima,
> Matsushima!

His poem won the contest.

"This is a true Zen poem. It does not use poetic language or images. There is no thinking in it. I am Matsushima, Matsushima is me.

"So in Zen there is no outside and no inside. There is only the one mind, which is just like this. This is the life of all the arts, and it is the life of Zen."

55. Plastic Flowers, Plastic Mind

One Sunday, while Seung Sahn Soen-sa was staying at the International Zen Center of New York, there was a big ceremony. Many Korean women came, with shopping bags full of food and presents. One woman brought a large bouquet of plastic flowers, which she smilingly presented to an American student of Soen-sa's. As quickly as he could, the student hid the flowers under a pile of coats. But soon another woman found them and, with the greatest delight, walked into the Dharma Room and put them in a vase on the altar.

The student was very upset. He went to Soen-sa and said, "Those plastic flowers are awful. Can't I take them off the altar and dump them somewhere?"

Soen-sa said, "It is your mind that is plastic. The whole universe is plastic."

The student said, "What do you mean?"

Soen-sa said, "Buddha said, 'When one mind is pure, the whole universe is pure; when one mind is tainted, the whole universe is tainted.' Every day we meet people who are unhappy. When their minds are sad, everything that they see, hear, smell, taste, and touch is sad, the whole universe is sad. When the mind is happy, the whole universe is happy. If you desire something, then you are attached to it. If you reject it, you are just as attached to it. Being attached to a thing means that it becomes a hindrance in your mind. So 'I don't like plastic' is the same as 'I like plastic'—both are attachments. You don't like plastic flowers, so your mind has become plastic, and the whole universe is plastic. Put it all down. Then you won't be hindered by anything. You won't care whether the flowers are plastic or real, whether they are on the altar or in the garbage pail. This is true freedom. A plastic flower is just a plastic flower. A real flower is just a real flower. You mustn't be attached to name and form."

The student said, "But we are trying to make a beautiful Zen Center here, for all people. How can I not care? Those flowers spoil the whole room."

Soen-sa said, "If somebody gives real flowers to Buddha, Buddha is happy. If somebody else likes plastic flowers and gives them to Buddha, Buddha is also happy. Buddha is not attached to name and form, he doesn't care whether the flowers are real or plastic, he only cares about the person's mind. These women who are offering plastic flowers have very pure minds, and their action is Bodhisattva action. Your mind rejects plastic flowers, so you have separated the universe into good and bad, beautiful and ugly. So your action is not Bodhisattva action. Only keep Buddha's mind. Then you will have no hindrance. Real flowers are good; plastic flowers are good. This mind is like the great sea, into which all waters flow—the Hudson River, the Charles River, the Yellow River, Chinese water, American water, clean water, dirty water, salt water, clear water. The sea doesn't say, 'Your water is dirty, you can't flow into me.' It accepts all waters and mixes them and all become sea. So if you keep the Buddha mind, your mind will be like the great sea. This is the great sea of enlightenment."

The student bowed deeply.

56. True Emptiness

One Sunday evening, after a Dharma talk at the Providence Zen Center, a student asked Seung Sahn Soen-sa, "What is true emptiness?"

Soen-sa said, "Are you asking because you don't know?"

The student said, "I don't know."

Soen-sa hit him.

The student said, "I don't understand why you hit me."

Soen-sa said, "The rocks in the stream and the tiles on the roof understand true emptiness. But you still don't understand it."

The student said, "What do you mean?"

Soen-sa said, "Put it all down!"

57. You Must Wake Up!

One Thursday evening, after a Dharma talk at the Cambridge Zen Center, a student said to Seung Sahn Soen-sa, "Last Sunday, when we were driving to Providence, you fell asleep in the car. Where did you go?"

Soen-sa said, "I will hit you thirty times."

The student said, "Oh, thank you very much."

Soen-sa said, "This question is not difficult. If you are thinking, you can't understand. If you cut off thinking, you will understand. So I hit you thirty times. Where is 'go'? Nowhere. Teach me."

"I wanted to know if you were dreaming. Do you mean that you weren't?"

"Do you dream?"

"Yes."

"Are you dreaming now?"

"No."

"No?!" (Laughter.)

"No."

"You are awake?"

"Now I'm only breathing."

"You are breathing in a dream."

"No."

"No? Then give me one awake sentence."

"The bamboo curtain behind you is yellow."

"No, it is dark."

"That's because it's behind you. If you turn around, you'll see it's yellow."

"Your head is a dragon, your tail is a snake."

"I said the bamboo is yellow. If you'd said, 'No good,' then . . ."

"I didn't say, 'No good.' You are attached to my words."

The student sighed.

Soen-sa said, "You must be careful not to be attached to my words. If I give a wrong answer, then you should hit me and say, 'You must wake up!' Okay?"

The student bowed.

58. More Ashes on the Buddha

December 15, 1974

Dear Ven. Satam,

Homage to the Three Precious Gems.

Thank you very much for your letter. I put my palms together and pray for you to make a greater effort and attain the great fruit as soon as possible.

Let us now discuss the *kong-ans*.

Regarding the first one about the man with the cigarette: the problem is that he doesn't say whether the Buddha and the ashes are the same or not, he just drops ashes on the statue. If, as you said in your letter, you ask him whether it comes out of existence or emptiness, he will just hit you. And he will then ask you, "Is this hit empty or does it exist?" If you open your mouth in reply, he will hit you again. What can you do?

When we admit that the Buddha statue is the Buddha statue and that the ashes are ashes, the problem is that Buddha said the Buddha-body permeates all the Dharma-realms and everything in the universe has Buddha-nature. So where can you drop the ashes if not on the Buddha-body? That is the disease of this person. How are you going to cure this disease?

Furthermore, he believes that the moment you open your mouth you are wrong. Buddha-nature is without words; the truth is without movement; the true state is where the way is cut off and mind is extinguished. So whatever you try to say, he will hit you. What can you do?

The second *kong-an* is: "The mouse eats cat-food, but the cat-bowl is broken. What does this mean?" Your answer was, "If you are hungry, take a meal and have a good rest." Your leg is itching, but you are scratching my leg. Do you think you will relieve the itching this way? You are trying to hit the moon with a stick. Your answer is 18,000 miles away from the correct one.

If the question were, "What is Buddha-nature?" or "What is Mind?" or "What is Dharma?", your answer would be 100% correct. But my question is: "The mouse eats cat-food but the cat-bowl is broken. What does this mean?" There is no special meaning outside the words. Don't be attached to the words. Don't be attached to your thinking or fall into emptiness. Just understand the clear meaning in the words: mouse, cat-food, bowl, and broken.

If you had a bell in front of you and I asked you, "What is this?", would you answer, "If you are hungry, have a good meal and a good rest"? This answer is not completely correct. The bell is to be rung, the watch is to tell time, the pen is to write with, and the book is for reading. Each has its own characteristics. When we act in accordance with the characteristics of each, there is the great truth as it is, the absolute truth apart from words. This is the realm of Big I. The question has four parts—mouse, cat-food, bowl, and broken.

These four parts combine, and there is a clear meaning behind the combination. Please try to grasp this meaning.

Here is a poem for you:

The candy peddler is ringing his bell,
and the child cries to its mother.
Money becomes candy and candy becomes money.
Money goes into the peddler's pocket,
and candy goes into the child's mouth and is sweet.

Dear Ven. Satam, what do you say? Take one step forward on top of the 100-foot pole. Make a fierce effort.

Here is another poem:

I traced the steps of the cow that has been long
    forgotten.
Having caught the harness,
I hope you will ride on the cow, playing the flute
    with no holes,
and enter your home village, where flowers bloom
    in the spring.

I sincerely hope that by keeping "What am I?" always and everywhere, you will attain the great fruit very soon.

S.S.

P.S. Please tell Dae Haeng to study well. I hope you will be good to him. If you can, translate this letter into English and send it back to me.

January 4, 1975

Dear Soen-sa-nim,

Thank you very much for your letter. Dae Haeng is now typing the translation of it, and I will try to mail it tomorrow.

After reading your kind instructions, I thought about the *kong-ans* as follows:

1. If the man hits me and asks, "Is this hit empty or real?", I will answer, "Ah ... ah ... ah." And I will hit him back and ask him whether my hit is empty or real. Of course,

I expect him to hit me back. That is his disease. He knows only form is emptiness, but he doesn't know emptiness is form. So . . .

2. My answer is, "The mouse eats cat-food, but the cat-bowl is broken."

I look forward to your kind instruction.

After the rain, the sky is bluer, and the sunshine falls brightly.

Thank you.

Yours respectfully,
Satam

January 10, 1975

Dear Ven. Satam,

Taking refuge in the Three Treasures—

Thank you for your letter and translation. I think you have been practicing hard and making great progress.

Now about the *kong-ans:*

1. To begin with, I will hit you thirty times. The problem is how to fix his mind and bring it to the realm of reality as it is. It is all right to hit him or ask him questions, but if you use the same words as he does, how are you different from him? You said in your letter that he understands "form is emptiness" but doesn't understand "emptiness is form." But these two statements are expressions of the same realm, which he has already transcended. He thinks he has reached the realm of "no form, no emptiness," and he is so strongly convinced of this that he will not listen to anyone. A statement such as "emptiness is form" means nothing to him. If you say, "Form is form, emptiness is emptiness," that might be better.

You must realize "What is this?" as soon as possible. That is why I hit you thirty times.

2. You are still attached to this *kong-an.* You must not turn into an ape. The real meaning is not in the words, but in what is meant by the combination of the four phrases: "mouse, cat-food, cat-bowl, and broken." Please try to grasp the meaning beyond the words.

As a man eats
an ape imitates him.
Acorns fall from the trees and roll down the slope.
Squirrels run after them.

Don't be an ape and run after acorns.

You said in your letter, "The sky is bluer after the rain, and the sunshine falls brightly." This is a very good sentence, but there is a pitfall in it. Please try to find this pitfall.

I hope you continue to do hard training and get the fruit as soon as possible and save all sentient beings.

Sincerely yours,
S.S.

59. The Story of Su Tung-p'o

Su Tung-p'o was one of the greatest poets of the Sung Dynasty. He was famous not only as a poet, but as an essayist, a painter, and a calligrapher as well. From an early age he had acquired great erudition in both the Confucian and the Buddhist classics. It is said that he knew the entire Buddhist canon by heart—some 84,000 volumes.

When he was twenty years old, Su Tung-p'o passed a high civil service examination and was appointed inspector of four provinces—the emperor's official representative, whose job it was to investigate all governmental operations in these districts. In the course of his travels, he would also visit famous Buddhist monasteries and, for his own pleasure, examine the monks and masters there. "So you know the Avatamsaka Sutra, hmm?" "Yes." "Well, tell me what doctrine is expounded in the last five lines of chapter forty-three?" Even the most learned masters hadn't memorized all the texts, so they couldn't answer his questions. Finally, he got disgusted with what he called the laziness and ineptitude of the monks, and lost interest in visiting them.

One day, however, Su Tung-p'o was told that in the Monastery of the Jade Springs there was a very learned Zen Master who would certainly be able to answer any question he could ask. So he mounted his horse and rode off to see for himself.

Traditionally, a man waited at the monastery gate for the keeper to come and escort him inside. But Su Tung-p'o opened the gate himself, rode in, went directly to the main lecture hall, and sat down with his back to the Buddha, waiting for someone to appear.

In a short time, the Master came in. He walked up to Su Tung-p'o and bowed respectfully. "Welcome, sir. It is a great honor to have such a high official as yourself visit our unworthy shrine. What, may I ask, is your name?"

"My name is Ch'eng." (Ch'eng means scales.)

"Mr. Scales? What a curious name!"

"I am called that because I can weigh all the eminent teachers in the land."

All at once the Master let out an ear-splitting yell. Then, with a faint smile, he said, "How much does *that* weigh?"

The answer to this was in none of the sutras. Su Tung-p'o was speechless. His arrogance crumbled, and he bowed respectfully to the Master. From this moment on, he began to devote himself to Buddhism.

Eventually Su Tung-p'o was reassigned to another province, where he came to know a Zen Master named Fo Yin. The two grew very close; people said they were like brothers. One day, Su Tung-p'o happened to visit Fo Yin in his official ceremonial robes. They were made of blue and green silk, with golden stitching, and were fastened by his great jade belt of office. They were very splendid robes.

As he entered the room, Fo Yin said, "Forgive me, great

sir, for the inadequate seating in my poor room. All I can offer you, I'm afraid, is a bare cushion on the bare floor."

Su Tung-p'o said, "Oh, that's all right. I'll just sit on you."

Fo Yin said, "I'll tell you what. Let me ask you a question. If you can give me a good answer, then you can use me as a chair. If not, you'll have to give me your jade belt."

"All right."

"It says in the Heart Sutra that matter is nothingness and nothingness is matter. Now if you use me as a chair, isn't this clinging to matter, without understanding its essential non-existence? But if all things don't really exist, what will you sit down on?"

Su Tung-p'o was stumped.

"You see, you're clinging even now. Do away with all discriminating thoughts. Then you'll understand."

Su Tung-p'o handed over his jade belt. From then on, he did Zen with great ardor. He meditated at all times, read many Zen books, and went to visit the Master whenever he could.

At the Temple of the Ascending Dragon there was a famous Zen Master named Chang Tsung. Su Tung-p'o went to him and said, "Please teach me the Buddha-dharma and open up my ignorant eyes."

The Master, whom he had expected to be the very soul of compassion, began to shout at him. "How dare you come here seeking the dead words of men! Why don't you open your ears to the living words of nature? I can't talk to someone who knows so much about Zen. Go away!"

Su Tung-p'o staggered out of the room. What had the Master meant? What was this teaching that nature could give and men couldn't?

Totally absorbed in this question, Su Tung-p'o mounted his horse and rode off. He had lost all sense of direction, so he let the horse find the way home. It led him on a path through the mountains. Suddenly he came upon a waterfall. The sound struck his ears. He understood. So this was what the Master meant! The whole world—and not only this world, but all possible worlds, all the most distant stars, the whole universe—was identical to himself. He got off his horse and bowed down to the ground in the direction of the monastery.

That evening Su Tung-p'o wrote the following poem:

> The roaring waterfall
> is the Buddha's golden mouth.
> The mountains in the distance
> are his pure luminous body.
> How many thousands of poems
> have flowed through me tonight!
> And tomorrow I won't be able
> to repeat even one word.

60. What Nature Is Saying to You

One Sunday evening at the Providence Zen Center, Seung Sahn Soen-sa told the story of Su Tung-p'o's enlightenment. Afterwards he said to his students:

"What do we learn from this story? That Zen teaches us to cut off all discriminating thoughts and to understand that the truth of the universe is ultimately our own true self. All of you should meditate very deeply on this. What is this thing that you call the self? When you understand what it is, you will have returned to an intuitive oneness with nature and will see that nature is you and you are nature, that nature is the Buddha, who is preaching to us at every moment. I hope that all of you will be able to hear what nature is saying to you."

One of Soen-sa's students pointed to a rock in the Dharma room and said, "What is that rock saying to you right now?"

Soen-sa said, "Why do you think it is saying anything?"

"Well, I can hear something, but I can't quite make out what it is."

"Why don't you ask the rock?"

"I already have, but I can't understand its language."

"That is because your mind is exactly like the rock." (Laughter from the audience.)

There was a minute of silence.

Soen-sa said, "Are there any more questions?"

More silence.

The student said, "If there are no questions, can you answer?"

Soen-sa said, "If there are no questions, then you are all Buddhas. And Buddhas don't need to be taught."

Another student said, "But we don't know we're Buddhas."

Soen-sa said, "That is true, you don't know. Fish swim in the water, but they don't know they are in water. Every moment you breathe in air, but you do it unconsciously. You would be conscious of air only if you were without it. In the same way, we are always hearing the sounds of cars, waterfalls, rain. All these sounds are sermons, they are the voice of the Buddha himself preaching to us. We hear many sermons, all the time, but we are deaf to them. If we were really alive, whenever we heard, saw, smelled, tasted, touched, we would say, 'Ah, this is a fine sermon.' We would see that there is no scripture that teaches so well as this experience with nature."

Another student asked, "Why do some see and others not?"

Soen-sa said, "In the past, you have sown certain seeds that now result in your encountering Buddhism. Not only that—some people come here only once, while others stay and practice very earnestly. When you practice Zen earnestly, you are burning up the karma that binds you to ignorance. In Japanese the word for 'earnest' means 'to heat up the heart.' If you heat up your heart, this karma, which is like a block of ice, melts and becomes liquid. And if you keep on heating it, it becomes steam and evaporates into space. Those people who practice come to melt their hindrances and attachments. Why do they practice? Because it is their karma to practice, just as it is other people's karma not to practice. Man's discriminating thoughts build up a great thought-mass in his mind, and this is what he mistakenly regards as his real self. In fact, it is a mental construction based on ignorance. The purpose of Zen meditation is to dissolve this thought-mass. What is finally left is the real self. You enter into the world of the selfless. And if you don't stop there, if you don't think about this realm or cling to it, you will continue in your practice until you become one with the Absolute."

The first student said, "What do you mean by the Absolute?"

Soen-sa said, "Where does that question come from?"

The student was silent.

Soen-sa said, "*That* is the Absolute."

"I don't understand."

"No matter how much I talk about it, you won't understand. The Absolute is precisely something you *can't* understand. If it could be understood, it wouldn't be the Absolute."

"Then why do you talk about it?"

"It is because I talk about it that you ask questions. That is how I teach, and how you learn."

61. It

May 18, 1975

Dear Soen-sa-nim,

This is the middle of the fourth day of my retreat. I got your letter yesterday when I was having a hard time. It is very difficult to sit this much without the teaching. I didn't realize before what the teaching is. It keeps me straight.

It is much harder alone because my Big I has to keep me straight, cutting through the small one constantly. There is no teacher.

This knot in my middle is the same as the edge—it is its own untying. When it unties, I breathe like the waves. There is no knot, no edge, nothing to untie or fall off of.

My only question is for me—What am I? All I can do is keep sitting.

Here's a question: If I never had it, how can I lose it?

Carol

P.S. I went to the ocean yesterday and saw why you named me Hae Mi—"Ocean Purity." I thought an edge to it when it's not even there.

So, I must find it.

9:30 A.M., 7th day

> As I crack the egg
> On the edge of the bowl
> I realize
> The bowl has no edge
> The egg has no shell
> No bowl
> No egg

Only love
Hae Mi

May 22, 1975

> No wall, no plant, no air, no sky
> Clinging to form
> Clinging to emptiness
> Stops the love
> We create this earth
> To teach us the love
> We are here on this earth
> To practice the love.

Hae Mi

May 27, 1975

Dear Carol,

Thank you for your three letters.

I was staying at the International Zen Center of New York, so I didn't see your letters until today, when I returned to Providence. I am sorry to be answering them late.

In your first letter, you speak about "no teacher." Don't worry about that. As I said to you before, if you want Big I and enlightenment, then only let your situation, condition, and opinions disappear. This is your true teacher. A teaching based on language alone is no good. If you are thinking, even a good teacher sitting in front of you will not help you. But if you cut off all thinking, then the dog's barking, the wind, the trees, the mountains, the lightning, the sound of the water—all are your teachers. So you must keep the complete don't-know mind. This is very necessary.

You said, "This knot in my middle is the same as the edge —it is its own untying. When it unties, I breathe like the waves. There is no knot, no edge, nothing to untie or fall off of." These words are not bad, not good. But you must not check your mind. This paragraph is about your condition. I already told you to throw away your condition.

If you say you haven't lost it, you have already lost it. If you want to find it, you won't be able to find it.

All people use it all the time.

But they don't understand it, because it has no name and no form.

It pierces past, present, and future, and it fills space.

Everything is contained in it.

It is apparent in everything.

But if you want to find it, it will go further and further away,

and if you lose it, it has already appeared before you.

It is brighter than sunlight, and darker than a starless night.

Sometimes it is bigger than the universe, sometimes smaller than the point of a needle.

It controls everything; it is the king of the ten thousand dharmas.

It is powerful and awesome.

People call it "mind," "God," "Buddha," "nature," "energy."

But it has no beginning or end, and is neither form nor emptiness.

If you want it, then you must ride the ship which has no hull;

you must play the flute with no holes;

you must cross the ocean of life and death.

You will then arrive at the village of "like this."

Within the village, you must find your true home, "just like this."

Then, when you open the door, you will get it.

It is only "it is."

In your second letter, you say, "no edge, no shell, no bowl, no egg." So how does love appear? Where does this love come from?

In your third letter, you say, "no wall, no plant, no air, no sky." So why do you say we make the earth? Why is love necessary? You say, "no wall, no plant, etc." But then you say, "We are here . . ." This is a contradiction. Put it all down. Put down "no . . . , no . . . , no . . ." Put down "love, love, love." Put down "we are here. . . ." Then you will understand the true earth, true we, and true love.

First you must find It. If you find it, you will have freedom and no hindrance. Sometimes its name is you, sometimes me, sometimes us, sometimes earth, sometimes love, sometimes hit, sometimes the tree has no roots and the valley has no echo, sometimes three pounds of flax, sometimes dry shit on a stick, sometimes like this, and sometimes just like this.

What is it?

See you soon,
S.S.

62. Small Love and Big Love

One Thursday evening, after a Dharma talk at the Cambridge Zen Center, a student said to Seung Sahn Soen-sa, "You always speak of thinking. I would like to know how the Way of the Heart fits into your teaching. In the Christian path it is said that without love, all attainments are worthless."

Soen-sa said, "There are two kinds of love. The first is small love. This is desire love, opposites love, attachment love. The second is big love. This is absolute love. It is freedom. If you have desire for yourself, your love is not true love. It is dependent on many conditions; if these change, you suffer. Suppose I love a girl very much, and she loves me. I go away to Los Angeles, and when I come back she has another boyfriend. My love changes to anger and hatred. So small love always contains suffering. Big love has no suffering. It is *only* love, absolute love, so there is no happiness, no suffering. This is Bodhisattva love."

"I was under the impression that Zen Masters don't care particularly about love."

"If I didn't love, why would I be teaching? Teaching is love. Hitting my students is true love."

"Why?"

"True teaching means true love. A true teacher sometimes gets angry, sometimes hits, sometimes does bad actions. Why? Because he loves his students very strongly. It is like a mother who loves her child very much, but the child doesn't listen to her good teaching. So sometimes it is necessary for the mother to get angry or hit her child. This is love action. There is no desire for herself; everything is for the child's sake, to teach it the true way. With big love, I have no desire for myself, I only give my love to other people. If I love you and you don't love me, that's okay. I will still give you as much love as if you loved me in return. If I love God and get bad karma in return, that's okay. I will not be angry at God, I will still love as much as before. So Big I is true love. It is only for all people."

"Do you love all people?"

"Of course! All people and all things. Okay, I will tell you a story. Once, long ago in China, there was a monk who went out begging and was on his way back to the temple. On the way, some robbers held him up and took all his money, food, and clothes. Then they threw him on his back and tied his hands and feet to the ground with braided strands of the long grass that was growing in the fields. He stayed there, naked, for hours. Finally, the emperor passed with his servants, on their way to the temple. He was shocked to see a naked man near the highway and went up to him to ask what had happened. The monk explained. The emperor said, 'Why haven't you just gotten up?' The monk said, 'Please untie the grass.' The emperor began to pull it up by the roots. 'Stop!' said the monk. 'You mustn't pull it up. Please untie it.' At this the emperor realized that the naked man was a great monk, whose love extended even to the grass in the fields. So he accompanied him to the temple and took him for his own teacher.

"So we see that big love doesn't kill anything. Most Christians think that killing humans is wrong, but killing animals is okay. 'Fishing—ah, it is very interesting.' Even killing grass is no good, so of course we mustn't kill fish or animals or people. But sometimes killing is big love. If one person wants to kill all people, then killing that person means saving all people. So Buddhist love is very wide love. You must understand this."

The student bowed deeply.

63. Does the Cat Have Buddha-Nature?

One evening, after a Dharma talk at the Cambridge Zen Center, a student pointed to Katz, the Zen Center cat, and said to Seung Sahn Soen-sa, "You said before that this cat doesn't say it's a cat, that it has don't-know mind. Is the cat enlightened? But if it is, why does Buddhism teach that only humans can attain enlightenment?"

Soen-sa said, "What is enlightenment?"

"I don't know."

"Enlightenment is not enlightenment. If someone says, 'I have attained enlightenment,' he is mistaken. Many students think, 'I want enlightenment! I want enlightenment!' With this kind of thinking, they will never attain enlightenment."

"The cat doesn't think enlightenment or no-enlightenment."

"The cat is just a cat. I ask you: Does the cat have Buddha-nature? If it has Buddha-nature, then it can attain enlightenment. If it has no Buddha-nature, no enlightenment."

"Hmmm . . . I don't know."

Soen-sa laughed and said, "Yah, don't-know is good. Very good."

64. Out of the Depths

June 13, 1975

Dear Soen-sa-nim,

I am sorry that I have not written, but I have nothing to say. I haven't been sitting well enough to answer your *kongans.* No games. I am feeling awful. My life is meaningless to me. I feel an indescribable anguish, all the time. I try and practice on my own, but somehow I am too weak to make any progress. I don't have any faith in my Buddha-nature. I really shouldn't be writing this letter, because a Zen Master should not have to deal with sick fools. Master Hearn told me to get in touch with you while he was gone, because you are a great Zen Master. I am afraid that I am not much of a man or Zen student, but anything you could tell me would help. I have contacted no one since he left or since I wrote to you because I believe you can't jump around to different masters.

I have no poems left in me, only doubt and anguish.

In gassho,
Steve

June 17, 1975

Dear Steve,

Thank you for your letter. You have written me many letters this year. These letters were not bad, not good. But the letter which you just sent me is a very wonderful letter. It is a true Zen letter. Thinking is only thinking. Suffering is only suffering. If you were to think, "I want my mind to become clear," this would be bad thinking. When you are suffering, you must only suffer.

So you must understand the true meaning of your letter. It told me the truth. You want to become enlightened. Without thinking, enlightenment is not possible. Thinking *is* enlightenment! An eminent teacher said, "Mind is constantly changing. This changing mind is itself entirely the truth. If you are not attached to your changing mind, then you will attain your true nature. Then you will understand that there is neither good nor bad."

You said that you are feeling very bad. If you *make* bad, it is bad. If you don't make bad, it is not bad. Don't make good or bad. Then everything will be good. You said, "I am not a good man, not a good Zen student." But if you understand good and bad, then good and bad have already disappeared. Please read the Heart Sutra once more. Then your mind will be clear. What is good? What is bad? You want to be a good Zen student; you want to be a good man. This is thinking. Put it down! Put it all down! If your mind is not clear, you must ask a tree or the sky to help you. Then the tree or the sky will give you a good answer.

If you are always checking your mind, that is very bad. Don't check your mind. You say that you have no faith in your Buddha-nature. I too have no faith in my Buddha-nature. And I have no faith in Buddha or God or anything. If you have no faith, you must *completely* have no faith. You must not believe in anything at all. Then your mind will become true emptiness. But this true emptiness is only a name. This true emptiness is before thinking. Before thinking is like this. It is very good that you don't have faith in your Buddha-nature. But when you see red, there is red; when you see white, there is only white. You must let go of both faith and non-faith. Things are only as they are.

I think that it would be good for you to visit other Zen Masters. If you have already made a strong decision in your mind about who is your teacher, then you can meet ten thousand other teachers and there will be no problem. And it would be good also to visit other meditation centers sometimes. Don't be concerned with the practice there. If you are free, then you can go and only sit by yourself, if necessary. You must always keep Big Mind.

I am sending you copies of some letters that I wrote to a student in New Haven. I hope that these letters will help you.

You mustn't worry about how your practice is, whether you are making progress or not, whether you are in anguish or not. All these things are not important. They are like clouds passing in front of the moon. You must not be attached to anything that appears in your mind. Then you will attain freedom thinking. No-attachment thinking is just like this.

I hope that you soon attain enlightenment and save all people from their suffering.

Yours sincerely,
S.S.

65. Funny

February 4, 1974

Dear Suzie, George, Roger, Alban, and Louise,

Thank you very much for your postcard. Are you all having a good time? Are you eating a lot? Doing hard training?

Your postcard said, "I hope you are having a good time." Thank you for helping us. We *are* having a good time. Much food, much talk, much visiting.

This world is very funny. In true nature, all things neither appear nor disappear. Yet people say that things have life and death. This is funny. Things are neither tainted nor pure. Yet people think that some things are good and some things are bad, some things are clean and some things are dirty. Things neither increase nor decrease. Yet people make circles and squares; they think that some things are long and some things are short. This is funny. People are attached to good karma and bad karma. They get happiness and suffering. They have past, present, and future; coming, going, and staying; East, West, North, and South. This is funny.

An eminent teacher once said, "Originally all things are empty." Yet you want to attain enlightenment. This is funny.

Put it down! Put it down! This is funny. What is there to put down?

Gatē, gatē, paragatē, parasamgatē, bodhi swaha!

A hungry child cries to its mother. A dog sniffs around in search of something to eat. As the sun sets behind the western mountain, the shadow of the pine tree grows longer and longer, and touches a distant wall.

See you soon.

Sincerely,
S.S.

66. The Story of Kyong Ho

Seventy-five years ago, when Seung Sahn Soen-sa's great-grandteacher, Zen Master Kyong Ho, was a young man, Korean Buddhism was very weak. Then Kyong Ho attained enlightenment and became the teacher of many great Zen monks. He is now known as the Patriarch of Korean Zen.

When Kyong Ho was nine years old, his father died. Since his mother was too poor to bring him up, she sent him to a temple and he became a monk. At the age of fourteen, he began to study the sutras. He was a brilliant student; he heard one and understood ten. Within a few years he had learned all he could from the sutra master, so he moved on to the great sutra temple Dong Gak Sa. There he advanced to the highest level. By the time he was twenty-three years old, he had mastered all the principal sutras. Soon many monks began to gather around him, and he became a famous sutra master.

One day, Kyong Ho decided to pay a visit to his first teacher. After a few days of walking, he passed through a small village. There were no people in the streets. Immediately he knew something was wrong, and he began to feel an overwhelming sense of disaster. He opened the door of one of the houses. There were five corpses lying on the floor, in various states of decomposition. He opened the door of the next house, and there were more corpses rotting on the floor. As he walked through the main street, dazed and terrified, he noticed a sign. "Danger: Cholera. If you value your life, go away."

This sign struck Kyong Ho like a hammer, and his mind became clear. "I am supposed to be a great sutra master; I already understand all of the Buddha's teachings. Why am I so afraid? Even though I understand that all things are transient, that life and death are aspects of the one reality, I am very attached to my body. So life is a hindrance, and death is a hindrance. What can I do?"

On the way home, Kyong Ho thought very deeply about these questions. Finally, he summoned all his students and said, "You have all come here to study the sutras, and I have been teaching you. But I know now that the sutras are only Buddha's words. They are not Buddha's mind. As many sutras as I have mastered, I still haven't attained true understanding. I can't teach you any more. If you wish to continue your studies, there are many qualified sutra masters who will be glad to teach you. But I have decided to understand my true self, and I will not teach again until I attain enlightenment."

All the students went away except one. Kyong Ho shut himself in his room. Once a day the student brought him food, leaving the platter outside the closed door. All day long, Kyong Ho sat or did lying-down Zen. He meditated on a *kong-an* which he had seen in a Zen book: "Zen Master Yong Un said, 'Before the donkey leaves, the horse has already arrived.' What does this mean?" "I am already as good as dead," he thought; "if I can't get beyond life and death, I vow never to leave this room." Every time he began to feel sleepy, he would take an awl and plunge it into his thigh.

Three months passed. During this time, Kyong Ho didn't sleep for a moment.

One day, the student went to a nearby town to beg for food. There he happened to meet a Mr. Lee, who was a close friend of Kyong Ho's. Mr. Lee said, "What is your Master doing nowadays?"

The student said, "He is doing hard training. He only eats, sits, and lies down."

"If he just eats, sits, and lies down, he will be reborn as a cow."

The young monk got very angry. "How can you say that? My teacher is the greatest scholar in Korea! I'm positive that he'll go to heaven after he dies!"

Mr. Lee said, "That's no way to answer me."

"Why not? How should I have answered?"

"I would have said, 'If my teacher is reborn as a cow, he will be a cow with no nostrils.'"

"A cow with no nostrils? What does that mean?"

"Go ask your teacher."

When he returned to the temple, the student knocked at Kyong Ho's door and told him of his conversation with Mr. Lee. As soon as he had finished, to his amazement, Kyong Ho opened the door and, with great luminous eyes, walked out of the room.

This is the poem which he wrote upon attaining the great enlightenment:

> I heard about the cow with no nostrils
> and suddenly the whole universe is my home.
> Yon Am Mountain lies flat under the road.
> A farmer, at the end of his work, is singing.

Soon afterward, he went to Zen Master Man Hwa for an interview. Man Hwa gave him Transmission and the Dharma name Kyong Ho, which means "Empty Mirror." He thus became the Seventy-fifth Patriarch in his line of succession. In turn, five great Zen Masters received the Transmission from him: Yong Son, Han Am, He Wol, Sa Wol, and Mang Gong, the teacher of Ko Bong, who was the teacher of Seung Sahn Soen-sa.

Just before Kyong Ho died, he wrote the following poem:

Light from the moon of clear mind
drinks up everything in the world.
When mind and light disappear,
what ... is ... this ...?

A moment after he had finished the poem, he was dead.

67. Bodhisattva Sin

One Thursday evening, after a Dharma talk at the New
Haven Zen Center, a student said to Seung Sahn Soen-sa,
"You say that sometimes a Bodhisattva will commit a wrong
action. What would be an appropriate occasion?"

Soen-sa said, "Come here." (A few giggles from the audience.)

The student came forward and kneeled in front of Soen-
sa. Soen-sa hit him. (Laughter.) Then he said, "Do you
understand?"

The student smiled and bowed.

Soen-sa said, "In our Temple Rules, it says, 'You have
taken the Five or the Ten Precepts. Know when to keep them
and when to break them, when they are open and when they
are closed.' The Precepts are very important: They are like a
sign pointing in the right direction, and without them it is
difficult to find the true way. But it is also important not to
be attached to the Precepts. No action is good or bad in itself.
Only the intention matters. So if you keep a Bodhisattva
mind, you may sometimes need to break the Precepts in
order to help others.

"For example, suppose you are walking in the woods and a rabbit crosses your path and runs off to the right. A few minutes later, a hunter comes along and asks you where the rabbit went. If you tell the truth, the rabbit may be killed. If you say nothing, the hunter may choose the right path. But if you tell a lie and send him off to the left, you will save the rabbit's life.

"Once Zen Master Kyong Ho was traveling with his student Zen Master Mang Gong. Mang Gong's leg began to hurt, so much so that when he finally sat down under a tree, he couldn't get up again. This was a big problem, since they had to be at a certain temple before nightfall, and there were still many miles to go.

"So Kyong Ho left Mang Gong under the tree and walked away. He crossed several fields until he came to some peasants at work. One of them was a girl of sixteen or seventeen. He went up to her, took her in his arms, and gave her a passionate kiss. The girl's father and the other peasants looked on in astonishment, which grew even greater when they noticed that Kyong Ho was a monk. Of course, they were outraged, and began to chase Kyong Ho across the fields. Kyong Ho headed right for the tree, shouting, 'Get up! Run for your life!' When Mang Gong saw him coming closer with a band of angry peasants behind him, he leaped up and ran away at full speed. They reached the temple before nightfall."

68. A Dharma Speech

Given by Seung Sahn Soen-sa
at Brown University
on March 18, 1974.

(*Holding up his Zen stick and hitting the table three times*) The Mahaparinirvana Sutra says, "All things are impermanent. This is the law of appearing and disappearing. When appearing and disappearing disappear, then this stillness is bliss."

The Diamond Sutra says, "All things that appear are transient. If we view all appearance as nonappearance, then we will see the true nature of all things."

The Heart Sutra says, "Form does not differ from emptiness; emptiness does not differ from form. That which is form is emptiness; that which is emptiness, form."

What is appearing and disappearing? What is impermanence and permanence? What is form and emptiness? In true stillness, in true nature, in true emptiness, there is no appearing or disappearing, no impermanence or permanence, no form or emptiness. The Sixth Patriarch said, "Originally there is nothing at all."

The sutra says, "When appearing and disappearing disappear, then this stillness is bliss." But there is no stillness and no bliss.

The sutra says, "If we view all appearance as nonappearance, then we will see the true nature of all things." But there is no true nature and no things.

The sutra says, "Form is emptiness, emptiness is form." But there is no emptiness and no form.

So when there is no thinking and no speech, already there is no appearing or disappearing, no impermanence or permanence, no form or emptiness. But to say that these things do not exist is incorrect. If you open your mouth, you are wrong.

Can you see colors, can you hear sounds, can you touch things? Is this form or is it emptiness? Tell me, tell me! If you say even one word, you are wrong. And if you say nothing, you are wrong. What can you do?

KATZ!!!

Appearing, disappearing—put it down! Impermanence, permanence—put it down! Form, emptiness—put it down!

Spring comes and the snow melts: appearing and disappearing are just like this. The east wind blows the rainclouds west: impermanence and permanence are just like this. When you turn on the lamp, the whole room becomes bright: all truth is just like this. Form is form, emptiness is emptiness.

Then what is your original face?

(Hitting the table) KATZ!!!

One two three four, four three two one.

69. The True Way

One morning, during Yong Maeng Jong Jin at the Providence Zen Center, a student walked into the interview room and bowed to Seung Sahn Soen-sa.

Soen-sa said, "What is the true way?"

The student shouted "KATZ!!!"

Soen-sa said, "That answer is neither good nor bad. It has

151

cut off all thinking, so there is no speech, no Buddha, no mind, no way. Tell me then: what is the true way?"

The student said, "The sky is blue."

Soen-sa said, "That's true enough, but it is not the way." Then, holding up his Zen stick, "What color is this?"

"Brown."

"Yes. When I ask you what color is the stick, you don't answer, 'The bell is yellow,' even though that's perfectly true. It would be scratching your left foot when your right one itches. It's the same when I ask you what is the true way and you answer, 'The sky is blue.'

"Go ask a child about the true way. A child will give you a good answer. Zen mind is children's mind. Children have no past or future, they are always living in the truth, which is just like this. When they are hungry, they eat; when they are tired, they rest. Children understand everything. So let me ask you again: what is the true way?"

The student stood up and bowed.

Soen-sa said, "This is the Great Way, the Buddha Way, the Tao. It is not the true way. Do you hear the sounds outside the window?"

"Yes."

"What are they?"

"Cars."

"Where are these cars driving?"

"Over there."

"What is the name over there?"

The student was confused and said nothing.

Soen-sa said, "It is Route 95. That is the true way. Hope Street is the true way. Doyle Avenue is the true way. The way is only the way. There is nothing beyond."

The student bowed and said, "I understand. Thank you."

Soen-sa said, "You're welcome. Now what is the true way?"

The student said, "Route 95 goes from Providence to Boston."

After he had returned to Cambridge, the student went up to two children—a six-year-old girl and a four-year-old boy —who were playing in the driveway by the Cambridge Zen Center. He asked the girl, "What is the true way?"

The girl pointed to Fayerweather Street.

He then asked the boy, "What is the true way?"

The boy gave him a fierce look, turned around, and walked away.

70. Sex Mind=Zen Mind?

One day a student of Seung Sahn Soen-sa's heard a Zen Master speak at Yale University. When he returned to the International Zen Center of New York, the student said to Soen-sa, "This Zen Master's teaching is a little strange. He says that sex mind is Zen mind, because when a man and woman are having sex, they lose their particular identities and become one. So he says that everyone should get married. Is this correct teaching?"

Soen-sa said, "Your mind when you are having sex and your mind when you are driving a car—are they the same or different?"

The student was silent.

Soen-sa said, "I will hit you thirty times."

"Why?"

"You must understand the true meaning of my hitting you. This Zen Master said that during sex you lose your Small I. This may be true. But outside conditions are taking away the Small I. When the outside conditions change, you again become Small I. When you are driving a car with a clear mind, you don't lose yourself. Outside and inside become one. Red light comes and you stop; green light comes and you go. But if you have sex on your mind, red comes and you don't understand red. You lose everything."

The student said, "So what is the difference between sex mind and Zen mind?"

Soen-sa said, "We can talk about three separate minds. The first is attachment mind. This is called losing your mind. Next is keeping one mind. The third is clear mind."

"What is losing your mind?"

"For example, you are standing in a train station and suddenly there is a loud whistle blast. You are startled out of yourself: no self, no world, only the whistle. This is losing your mind. Or if you haven't eaten for three days and then someone gives you food, you gobble it down without thinking. There is only the eating. Or when you are having sex, there is only the good feeling, the absorption in the other person. This is losing your mind. But afterwards, when you stop having sex, your small mind is just as strong as ever. All these actions are attachment actions. They come from desire and end in suffering."

"What is keeping one mind?"

"When somebody is reciting a mantra, there is only the mantra. He sees good, and there is only *Om mani padme hum;* he sees bad, and there is only *Om mani padme hum.* Whatever he does, whatever he sees, there is only the mantra."

"Then what is clear mind?"

"Clear mind is like a mirror. Red comes, and the mirror is red; white comes, and the mirror is white. When all people are sad, I am sad; when all people are happy, I am happy. The mind that only tries to help all people is clear mind. So the mind that is lost in desire is small mind. One mind is empty mind. Clear mind is big mind, which is infinite time and infinite space."

"It's still not completely clear to me. Would you please give me another example?"

"Okay. Suppose a man and a woman are having sex. They have lost their minds and they are very very happy. Just then, a robber breaks in with a gun and says, 'Give me money!' All their happiness disappears and they are very afraid. 'Oh help me, help me!' This is small mind. It is constantly changing, as outside conditions change.

154

"Next, somebody is doing mantra. This is one mind. His mind is not moving at all. There is no inside or outside, only true emptiness. The robber appears. 'Give me money!' But the person is not afraid. Only *Om mani padme hum, Om mani padme hum.* 'Give me money or I'll kill you!' He doesn't care. Already there is no life and no death. So he is not in the least afraid.

"Next is clear mind. This person always keeps Bodhisattva mind. The robber appears. 'Give me money!' This person says, 'How much do you want?' 'Give me everything!' 'Okay'—and he gives the robber all his money. He is not afraid. But his mind is very sad. He is thinking, 'Why are you doing this? Now you are all right, but in the future you will have much suffering.' The robber looks at him and sees that he is not afraid, that there is only motherly compassion on his face. So the robber is a little confused. The person has given him money and is now teaching him the correct way. This is true Zen mind."

The student bowed deeply and said, "Thank you very much."

Soen-sa said, "There are four difficult things in this life. The first is to receive a human body. The second is to encounter the Dharma. The third is to meet a keen-eyed Zen Master. The fourth is to attain enlightenment. Number three is very important. A Zen Master may not be deeply enlightened; he may not be a good teacher. If you meet the wrong Zen Master, you will go the wrong way. It is like one blind man leading another blind man into a ditch. So I hope you will be able to tell the difference between a keen-eyed lion and a blind dog."

The student said, "How can I tell the difference?"

Soen-sa said, "Now it is time for breakfast."

The student bowed.

71. Keen-Eyed Lions and Blind Dogs

The next morning, the student said to Soen-sa, "You were talking yesterday morning about different kinds of teachers. How can I recognize a keen-eyed Zen Master?"

Soen-sa said, "It is difficult if you stay only in one place. You should go around and hear many Zen Masters. Then you will soon understand. In the Avatamsaka Sutra, there is a story about a young boy who studied with fifty-three teachers. He would learn what he could from one teacher, and then travel on to another. Finally, he met Manjushri, the Bodhisattva of wisdom. Manjushri asked him, 'What have you learned from these fifty-three teachers?' The boy said this teacher had taught him this, and that teacher had taught him that. Manjushri hit him. Everything he had learned disappeared. As soon as he realized this, he decided to begin his travels again in search of a teacher. At that moment, Manjushri, who himself had disappeared, reached out across ten thousand worlds and touched the boy on the forehead. 'This beginner's mind,' he said, 'is the true mind of enlightenment.' Upon hearing this, the boy became enlightened.

"Some people study Zen for five or ten years without attaining enlightenment. They become very attached to their teacher, and this teacher cannot help them understand. If you study with only one teacher, even if he is a great teacher, it is difficult to meet Manjushri. So Zen students should travel from teacher to teacher until they find a keen-eyed Zen Master. This is very important."

The student said, "But how will I know?"

Soen-sa said, "At first you may not know. But if you practice Zen for a while and listen to many Zen Masters, you will soon understand what is correct teaching and what is not. If you don't taste sugar, you can't understand sweet; if you don't taste salt, you can't understand salty. No one can taste for you. You have to do it yourself."

"But aren't all Zen Masters enlightened?"

"There are different levels of enlightenment. There is first enlightenment, original enlightenment, final enlightenment. First enlightenment is attaining true emptiness. Original enlightenment is attaining 'like this.' Final enlightenment is 'just like this.' "

"Would you please explain some more?"

"Okay. Here is an apple. If you say it is an apple, you are attached to name and form. But if you say it is not an apple, you are attached to emptiness. So is this an apple or not? If you hit the floor or shout KATZ, this is a first-enlightenment answer. If you say, 'The sky is blue, the grass is green,' or 'The apple is red, the wall is white,' you are giving a 'like this' answer. But if you take a bite of the apple, your answer is 'just like this.' In the same way, you would ring the bell or open the book and read it. So first enlightenment, original enlightenment, and final enlightenment all have different answers. Some Zen Masters do not make these distinctions. Some only understand KATZ or silence. Some distinguish between KATZ and 'like this,' but don't understand 'just like this.' A keen-eyed Zen Master distinguishes among the three kinds of enlightenment. But he uses all three kinds with perfect freedom."

"The Zen Master I heard in New Haven said that there is no such thing as complete enlightenment. He said that you can never finish. Is that correct?"

"Buddha said, 'All beings are already enlightened.' An eminent teacher said, 'Without thinking, just like this is Buddha.' Without thinking is clear mind. So if you keep a clear mind, then any action is just like this. To say that you attain more enlightenment, more, more, more, is thinking.

Thinking is desire. Desire is suffering. So Zen Master Nam Chan said, 'Everyday mind is the Way.' "

The student said, "I have one more question. You said that a keen-eyed Zen Master distinguishes three separate kinds of enlightenment. But isn't Zen mind precisely the mind that doesn't create distinctions? Didn't the Third Patriarch say, 'The Great Way is not difficult for those who do not discriminate'? "

Soen-sa said, "First enlightenment, original enlightenment, final enlightenment—are these the same or different?"

The student thought for a moment, then smiled and said, "The wall is white, the rug is blue."

Soen-sa said, "You are attached to color."

"*You* are attached to color!"

"The dog runs after the bone."

"Then are they the same or different?"

Soen-sa said, "The wall is white, the rug is blue."

The student smiled.

72. Original Sound, Original Body

October 12, 1974

Dear Soen-sa-nim,

Hello from Cambridge! I hope you enjoy the enclosed "Zen Comics"—perhaps they're good to practice English with.

Things here are fine. "What am I?" grows and grows. . . . The yoga school starts Saturday. I have two classes to begin with, one on Saturday mornings, the other a special class of mostly professors and their wives and friends during the week. Each class will be two hours—body movements, breathing, and instructions on cleansing and diet, followed by an introduction to Zen sitting. At first only a half-hour sitting, then longer periods of time on the cushion. Dae Ja will give a yoga class for women, Jonny will give a yoga class too. It will be called the Cambridge Zen Center Institute of Hatha Yoga.

A friend of mine will bring two very wealthy people to speak to us soon. They have been generous with their time and money for others—perhaps they will help us as well.

Yesterday I had a very good interview for a teaching job that may be very helpful for us. What is unusual about the position is that I would be a *university* professor, which means that I would not be in any special subject (e.g., psychology, philosophy, etc). It would allow me to teach whatever I want (even Dharma). It pays much money, which would make supporting the Zen Center easier. But it is hard to get—especially since most professors are not ready to let someone come in at a high level to teach Zen, yoga, etc. If they give me the job, they will have to let me teach what I like.

A few questions:

1) I have heard a sound "in my head" while meditating for a few years now. But now it has become very strong and comes within a few minutes of sitting. It sounds like many crickets or a loud sea shell—very pleasant. It comes in response to "What am I?" Do I watch it like a tiger? disappear into it? forget it?*

2) Regarding rebirth: To be honest, I have no *actual experience* (or don't know it) of ever having been alive before: nor do I know what happens upon death to the physical body. The Buddhist theory of rebirth is very intelligent and plausible, but I have no *direct* awareness of this truth. Two very

---

*Does this have anything to do with Avalokiteshvara Bodhisattva's method of separating hearing from outside sounds and turning inwards to hear the self-nature?

psychic people told me I was Oriental once before, and since I was a little child I have always been *very* comfortable with the Oriental style of living. Once on LSD I felt that I had been a very wild primitive hunter-type person in Mongolia; but I did not take this for an *actual* picture of a past life.

I do feel more "close" to the ideas of oneness and emptiness in Buddhism, but this is because of a *little* experience of such possibilities on LSD. Who is there to be reborn? It is not a constant, since *everything* changes. Many people at the Zen Center and in Cambridge seem very confident about rebirth. I don't know! It is not absolutely necessary for my practice, because even if this were "my" one and only life I would sit Zen anyway. Can you help me? I certainly trust that Buddha, the Patriarchs, and yourself are not liars. But I need to know from within myself too.

I must also admit that my "little I" hates the *kong-an* method. Of all the spiritual methods—yoga, chanting, mantra, breathing, etc.—it is the only one that "little I" really dislikes. My professor-mind moves like a car on square wheels and flies like a plane with noodles for wings. It is good medicine for me! Come back soon and laugh with us again.

May your Buddha-teaching yield rootless skinless nonfruit in America.

Love,
Byon Jo

October 21, 1974

Dear Byon Jo,

Thank you for your letter and book. The book is very good, and I will read it and learn Zen-English words. I am glad that you have begun the yoga school and I hope it grows every day and becomes the number-one yoga school in the U.S.

Now some Americans are coming to Tal Mah Sah to sit Zen. They are hearing the teachings of the Chogye school (our way) for the first time, and they like our kind of Zen very much. Some of them want to become our students and will come to the Cambridge Zen Center. If they come to Cambridge, you must help them.

It is good if rich people come to the Zen Center, but it is better if our students work hard and make enough money to buy a house. This way is a better way.

I hope you soon get the job and help all people. Many people are attached to name and form, and if you are a professor they will listen to you in a different way. So it will be easier for you to help them. I hope you get the job, help all people, and become a good professor.

To answer your question about sound: this is original sound. If you are very quiet, you will hear original sound; but if you become attached to this sound, it will grow very loud, and this is no good. Only keep "What am I?" Then the sound will be "What am I?" Then sound will be no sound, no sound will be sound. Then you will understand your true self. This is your true self.

Your true self has no inside, no outside.

Sound is clear mind; clear mind is sound.

Sound and hearing are not separate. There is only sound.

I ask you—now you have a body: does it exist or is it emptiness?

How many colors are there in the rainbow?

One person says there are five colors, another says seven, another says twelve, another says thirty, another says a hundred. Which one is correct?

Originally the rainbow has no color.

Buddhism separates lives into past, present, and future. Christianity has no past lives, only present and future. Taoism has no past or future, only the present. Which is correct?

The Heart Sutra says that "form is emptiness, emptiness is form." If you are attached to name and form, then all things appear and disappear. But if you cut off all thinking, then all things do not appear and do not disappear.

Buddhism says there is rebirth. Is this correct or not correct?

If you say "correct," I will hit you thirty times.

If you say "not correct," I will still hit you thirty times. Why?

Already you understand.

The cat likes the mouse.

When you don't make "little I," and you don't make "professor," and you are not attached to the *kong-an* method, all thinking returns to your true self and your mind becomes clear. Mind is like a blackboard. You make pictures on it like "little I," "professor," "Zen student," etc. When you erase it, everything disappears. At first everything disappears; then you must draw only a Bodhisattva picture. Bodhisattva means no desire for myself, only for all people. So I hope that you PUT IT DOWN

PUT IT DOWN

PUT IT ALL DOWN

Here is a poem for you:

Form body and thinking body—where do they
come from?
Before thinking there is no name and no form,
only infinite time and infinite space.
The children chase butterflies with a net.
Wind comes and an apple falls to the ground.

I hope you soon get enlightenment and become a great man.

See you soon.
S. S.

73. The Story of Mang Gong

Zen Master Mang Gong, Seung Sahn Soen-sa's grand-teacher, became a monk when he was a young boy, and for several years studied the Mahayana sutras at Dong Hak Sa temple. One day, when he was thirteen years old, there was a great ceremony to mark the beginning of the long vacation. The sutra master got up and said, "You must all study very hard, learn Buddhism, and become like great trees, from which temples are built, and like large bowls, able to hold many good things. The sutra says, 'Water becomes square or round according to the shape of the container it is put in. In the same way, people become good or bad according to the friends they have.' Always have the Buddha in mind and keep good company. Then you will become great trees and containers of Dharma. This I sincerely wish."

The next speaker was Zen Master Kyong Ho, who happened to be visiting the temple. He was already known all over Korea as a very great Zen Master and, clothed in rags, with long hair and a long, thin beard, he was a striking figure among the neat, shaven-headed monks. He said, "All of you are monks. Monks are free of petty personal attachments and live only to serve all people. Wanting to become a great tree or container of Dharma will prevent you from being a true teacher. Great trees have great uses; small trees have small uses. Good and bad bowls can all be used in their own way. None are to be discarded. Keep both good and bad friends.

You mustn't reject anything. This is true Buddhism. My only wish for you is that you free yourselves from all conceptual thinking."

Everyone was filled with deep admiration. As the Zen Master walked out of the Dharma room, Mang Gong ran after him and pulled at his robe. Kyong Ho turned around and said, "What do you want?"

Mang Gong said, "I want to become your student. Please take me with you."

Kyong Ho shouted at him to go away, but the boy would not leave. Then he said, with great severity, "You are only a child. You are incapable of learning Buddhism."

Mang Gong said, "People may be young or old, but is there youth or old age in Buddhism?"

Kyong Ho said, "You bad boy! You have killed and eaten the Buddha! Come along now."

He took the boy to Chung Jung Sa temple, introduced him to the abbot, and left him there.

Mang Gong studied hard for the next five years. One day, when he was eighteen, he heard the *kong-an*: "The ten thousand dharmas return to the One: where does the One return to?" Immediately he was plunged into the great doubt. He couldn't eat or sleep or think of anything but that one question. All day long, and far into the night, he would keep the question in his mind, wherever he was, whatever he was doing.

One day, as he was sitting Zen, a large hole appeared in the wall which he was facing. He could see the whole landscape! Grass, trees, clouds, and the blue sky appeared through the wall with total clarity. He touched the wall. It was still there, but it was transparent like glass. He looked up, and he could see right through the roof. At this Mang Gong was filled with an inexpressible joy. Early the next morning, he went to see the Zen Master, rushed into his room, and announced, "I have penetrated the nature of all things. I have attained enlightenment."

The Master said, "Oh, have you? Then what is the nature of all things?"

Mang Gong said, "I can see right through the wall and the roof, as if they weren't there."

The Master said, "Is this the truth?"

"Yes. I have no hindrance at all."

The Master took his Zen stick and hit Mang Gong on the head. "Is there any hindrance now?"

Mang Gong was astonished. His eyes bulged, his face flushed, and the walls became solid again. The Master said, "Where did your truth go?"

"I don't know. Please teach me."

"What *kong-an* are you working on?"

" 'Where does the One return?' "

"Do you understand One?"

"No."

"You must first understand One. What you saw was an illusion. Don't be led astray by it. With more hard work on your *kong-an,* you will soon understand."

Mang Gong came out of this interview with renewed aspiration. For the next three years he meditated continually on the great question. Then, one morning that was no different from other mornings, he sang the words of the morning bell chant: "If you wish to understand all Buddhas of the past, present, and future, you must perceive that the whole universe is created by the mind alone." Having sung this, he hit the great bell. Suddenly his mind opened, and he understood that all Buddhas dwell in a single sound.

Dizzy with joy, Mang Gong ran to the Dharma room and kicked the monk who used to sit next to him. The monk cried out and said, "Are you crazy?"

Mang Gong said, "This is Buddha-nature!"

"Have you attained enlightenment?"

"The whole universe is one. I am Buddha!"

During the next year, Mang Gong kicked and hit many other monks and became very famous. People said, "He is a free man. He has no hindrance at all."

One day, a year later, there was an important ceremony at which Kyong Ho was present. Mang Gong went to his room thinking, "This Zen Master and I are the same. We have both attained enlightenment. He is Buddha, so am I. But since he was my first teacher I will bow to him, just as an ordinary monk would do."

After Mang Gong had bowed, Kyong Ho said, "Welcome. It's been a long time since I've seen you. I heard that you have attained enlightenment. Is that true?"

Mang Gong said, "Yes, Master."

"Wonderful. Now let me ask you a question." Kyong Ho picked up a fan and a writing brush and put them in front of Mang Gong. "Are these the same or different?"

Mang Gong said, "The fan is the brush; the brush is the fan."

For the next hour, with grandmotherly compassion, Kyong Ho tried to teach Mang Gong his mistake. But Mang Gong wouldn't listen. Finally Kyong Ho said, "I have one more question for you. In the burial ceremony there is a verse that says, 'The statue has eyes, and its tears silently drip down.' What does this mean?"

Mang Gong was stunned. He could find nothing to say. Suddenly, Kyong Ho shouted at him, "If you don't understand this, why do you say that the fan and the brush are the same?" In great despair, Mang Gong bowed and said, "Forgive me."

"Do you understand your mistake?"

"Yes, Master. What can I do?"

"Long ago, when Zen Master Jo-ju was asked if a dog had Buddha-nature, he said, 'No!' What does this mean?"

"I don't know."

Kyong Ho said, "Always keep the mind that doesn't know and you will soon attain enlightenment."

Mang Gong understood what a great gift this teaching was. For the next three years, he did very hard training and always kept don't-know mind. One day he heard the great bell ring and understood Jo-ju's answer. He returned to Kyong Ho, bowed, and said, "Now I know why the Bodhisattva faces away: because sugar is sweet and salt is salty."

74. Mang Gong Explains His KATZ

Once Zen Master Mang Gong was staying in Yang San Tong Do Sa temple with Zen Master He Wol. It was time for lunch. All the monks sat down and were served. Everyone was waiting for the *chuk-pi** to be struck so that they could begin eating. Suddenly He Wol shouted "KATZ!!!" Everyone was startled and confused. They looked over at He Wol. With total unconcern, he was only eating.

So everyone began to eat. But they were thinking, "Why did the Master shout?" "What did that mean?" "Why can't I understand what just happened?" Finally lunch was over, and the bowls were cleaned, dried, and wrapped in their covering cloths. The *chuk-pi* was struck, and everyone stood up. Suddenly Mang Gong shouted "KATZ!!!" Again, everyone was startled and confused.

Afterwards, one monk came to Mang Gong and asked him what all this meant. Mang Gong said, "I'm sorry, but I can't tell you." Then another monk came; then two, then three. They bowed and said, "Please, Master, teach us."

Finally, Mang Gong said, "I don't like to open my mouth. But since you have asked me, and since you are all sincere in your desire to understand, I will explain." Then, suddenly, Mang Gong shouted "KATZ!!!" and walked away.

---

*A wooden clapper used to signal the beginning and end of meditation periods and meals.

75. The Transmission of No-Mind

One Thursday evening, after a Dharma talk at the Cambridge Zen Center, a student asked Seung Sahn Soen-sa, "In the Zen tradition, what is the teaching about grace, or the transmission of no-mind from teacher to student?"

Soen-sa said, "How can this no-mind be transmitted? What is there to transmit? Once Buddha was staying at Vulture Peak. Every day he would deliver a long sermon to his disciples. One day there were twelve hundred people assembled to hear his Dharma. He sat down in front of them and was silent. One minute passed, then five minutes, then ten minutes. Finally Buddha held up a flower. Only Mahakashyapa understood and smiled. Buddha then said, 'I have the true Dharma, and I transmit it to you.' But later an eminent teacher said, 'Buddha is crazy. Everybody already has the true Dharma, so how can Buddha transmit it to him alone? This is like selling dog-meat and advertising it as filet mignon.' In Zen, Transmission means only that a Zen Master certifies that you have already attained enlightenment. He tests your mind to see whether you understand or not. If you have attained enlightenment, then he transmits his teaching-style to you."

A second student said, "You say that a Zen Master tests a student's enlightenment. But if all people already have the true Dharma, if they already have Buddha-nature, how can someone *not* be enlightened?"

Soen-sa said, "Your hair is very dark. Why is it dark?"

"It's dark. Just that."

"You are attached to dark."

"But it's dark!"

"The Heart Sutra says that there are no eyes and no color. So where does dark come from?"

"I don't know."

"You don't know? I will hit you!"

"It comes from my mind."

"Your mind? Where is your mind?" (Laughter from the audience.) "You don't know dark, yah?"

The student was silent.

"You don't know everything."

The student was still silent.

Soen-sa said, "*This* is how a Zen Master tests someone's mind." (Loud laughter.) "Everybody sees that your hair is dark, but they don't understand. Everybody has Buddha-nature, but they don't understand. So having your mind checked is very necessary."

76. Inside the Cow's Belly

One morning Seung Sahn Soen-sa gave the following Dharma talk at the Providence Zen Center:

"A long time ago, after breakfast, an eminent Zen Master took three grains of rice and turned them into a tiny cow. At first this cow was very small and very hungry. She looked around the table and saw a needle and began to eat it. She proceeded to eat every object she could fit into her mouth. The cow soon began to grow. The more she ate, the bigger she became. Soon she was big enough to eat the eminent Zen Master, which she did with great relish.

"She ate up the entire kitchen and went into the Dharma room. She ate the *moktak*; she ate the incense; she ate the Buddha! She was still very hungry, so she ate the whole temple and all the buildings surrounding it.

"The cow grew and grew. She never had to shit, so everything she ate just made her that much bigger. Although it was a frightening experience to be eaten by this cow, it did not harm anyone physically.

"But soon there was much suffering. Once inside the cow's belly, people became attached to name and form. They formed conceptions of good and bad, time and space, light and darkness. The cow continued to eat and eat. She ate all the mountains and rivers, and all the Bodhisattvas, eminent teachers, and Buddhas.

"So all infinite time and space, the entire universe, was eventually contained within the cow's belly.

"Now you are all inside the cow's belly, where all things appear and disappear. You are all attached to name and form. Outside the cow there is no suffering; nothing appears and nothing disappears.

"How can you get out?"

77. Today Is Buddha's Birthday. The Sun Is Shining.

May 10, 1973

Dear Soen-sa-nim,

Thank you for the acupuncture books. And thank you for the beautiful letter.

Today is Buddha's birthday. We have special incense on the altar. Last night Professor Pruden came for dinner. He ate a lot of tempura and salad. We did some Buddha's birthday chanting for him and he looked very happy.

I utter the lion's roar and kill all the Buddhas, all the eminent teachers, and all people. So all the mountains fall, and the seas become empty.

What is it that utters the lion's roar? I don't know. KATZ!!! Today is Buddha's birthday. The sun is shining.

Bobby

May 14, 1973

Dear Bobby,

How are all of you? I am very grateful to you for your letter and for the books on *The Teaching of Buddha.*

It is wonderful that you celebrated Buddha's birthday. Thank you. I am happy to hear that you had Professor Pruden over to dinner.

Your letter was very good, which means that you have been sitting Zen sincerely while I have been away.

About the sentence, "I utter the lion's roar": even though you have killed all the Buddhas, all eminent teachers, and all people, you fall into hell like an arrow. Since there is originally nothing, it is not necessary to kill or let the mountains fall and the seas empty.

"I don't know. KATZ!!!" This, too, is very fine. But how can you separate red from white and top from bottom, since there is no head or tail, no eye or ear in these words?

So even if you pass beyond infinite time, you still can't attain Buddhahood.

Coming out of that place, you said that today is Buddha's birthday and the sun is shining.

How can I praise you enough? The truth is just like this.

But even though you have told the truth, if you don't understand that fine hairs are growing on the bone of space, you still don't know your true self. What can you do?

> The blue mountains stand unmoving;
> the white clouds float back and forth.

See you soon.
S. S.

78. Dok Sahn and His Stick

Zen Master Dok Sahn was famous for answering questions by hitting the questioner with his Zen stick. One day he went into a temple to give a talk. He stood on a platform in front of the people, holding his Zen stick, and said, "Today there will be no questions and answers. If you ask me a question, I will hit you thirty times."

A student walked up to him and bowed. Dok Sahn hit him thirty times.

"Why did you hit me?" asked the student. "I just bowed, I didn't ask any questions."

Dok Sahn said, "Where do you come from?"

The student said, "The East."

Dok Sahn said, "Before you leave the East, I will hit you thirty times."

So Dok Sahn hit him thirty times. The student bowed and returned to his seat.

One day a student came to Dok Sahn and bowed. Dok Sahn immediately hit him. The student said, "Where is my mistake?"

Dok Sahn said, "I'm not going to wait for you to open your mouth."

Another time a monk came into Dok Sahn's room. He was clear-eyed and confident. He understood that Dok Sahn only hit people, so he was ready to be the first to strike. He raised his hand, but Dok Sahn had already raised his stick. "What is this? Your action is not permitted!"

The student was confused and began to walk out of the room. Dok Sahn hit him across the back. The student looked up, and Dok Sahn shouted "KATZ!!!"

The student froze. Dok Sahn said, "Is this all the capital you have?"

The student bowed and said, "I am sorry."

Dok Sahn patted him on the back, saying, "Good, good."

So Dok Sahn hit many students, and opened many minds.

79. All Things Are Your Teachers

January 7, 1975

Dear Soen-sa-nim,

How does it go in Rhode Island and Cambridge?

In April, Song Ryong will go to Asia, and then I think I will leave here. A Ceylonese monk, Ananda (a monk for thirty years), wishes me to help him open a center in my home town. But I don't feel ready. There is little in any of the scriptures that this person does not understand, or in *kong-ans*; but it seems that understanding is not important at all—at least the understanding put in words. It is only important to see what is, to destroy or not allow to arise any discrimination of inner and outer, of holy or evil; then one can see clearly from the aspect of eternity, of no time. But I should be given thirty blows for this way of speaking.

Now for this problem:

Increasingly, for the last two years, I've been coming out

of emptiness, and more and more see that I am the world and the world is me. As I think, so is the world, and as I act, so I create the world around me. Since seeing this, more clearly, every day I see a duty to teach others: to teach how each person creates his own heaven and hell, how he/she, through hatred and anger, creates a world of hatred and anger.

I can no longer live for myself. I must help and show others. But I lack the *power* to help others; they do not listen —not because I don't understand, but because my understanding has not become me. But now, I've dropped off all understanding because when one acts *from a point of understanding,* that understanding is still separate. When understanding is *dropped,* real understanding of there is nothing to understand comes. But even this must be dropped. So how can one tell someone who is desperate for truth, for God, for a ceasing of pain that all that must be done is to stop seeking?

Every day I see my responsibility growing, not as an idea, but in every day I see more ways in which I should help, but I lack a way to do it, for it is not clear how to help or to have people listen.

Because I see my responsibilities more clearly every day, I have become much more careful in how I act—more gentle, more involved—and not avoiding things that require activity, such as working to pay off debts, feeding homeless animals. But also, I get so very angry when I see other people avoiding their responsibilities: running out on debts, or in the name of spiritual detachment leaving their wives and children claiming it doesn't matter—it's all the same, everything is one. Bullcrap! They are just lazy and running away from the world, clinging to a false peace of nonaction. They have no order in their lives and they think they have some deep understanding (much like your *kong-an* of the man knocking ashes on the Buddha). And they make me so angry because they cannot see how their way of acting, of avoiding responsibility, hurts and causes pain in others, and I see no way to do anything.

Or else, I see a very ambitious person who hurts many people in order to get his dream realized, but he doesn't care about them, he cares only for his dream.

I feel frustrated, for I cannot "get to these people" to

show them how they create pain in the world and damage to themselves. So I continue to sit, to clear my own mind further and maybe to see a way to teach these people to stop hurting others and themselves through their ambition, or irresponsibility, or hatred, or their ideals. And my own anger at being able to do nothing makes me ill. This is no new problem. It has been with me since I was eighteen—about fourteen years.

This leads to the second problem. When Hearn leaves in April, it is not clear what I should do, except I do not want to stay here. None of the Zen Masters in Los Angeles seem very good, and none of the centers have a strong practice—people do what they want, have little discipline, and sit very little. Being around these people is difficult, because I cannot convince them of the value of sitting.

1. Should I go on a 100-day retreat on my brother's land in the desert in Arizona?

2. Find a Zen Master in Japan at a center or monastery where they have a strong practice?

3. Establish a Center with Ananda in my home town before I am ready?

4. Come to Providence or Cambridge to study with you, who I feel have a good understanding? But I have difficulty in understanding your Zen talk (though I feel very attracted to you), for I find no correspondence to your words as you usually talk them in my own mind, while, for example, I find Song Ryong easy to understand.

Can you answer in non-Zen talk, or Zen talk if necessary?

It is easy to say that when the time comes, it will be clear what I should do. But in this case it appears this is not true, for I've wanted to leave here almost since I first came, but no alternative seemed good, and none seems good now. So here I stay, constantly getting into small fights with my teacher about his dishonesty and the lack of practice here.

Slowly, there has been some increase in the practice here, but it is very slow. Also, since there is no practice here, I sit by myself for five hours a day, and this is not too good, because when all the effort comes from oneself, that self gets very big and strong and it becomes harder to let go, to drop things. It is all self power and little "other power." While if practice is strong, much of the effort to sit becomes merely a matter of doing what must be done, and the self does not become stronger and stronger. Self-directed practice eventually produces the same results, but it is slower, especially since there is no real Zen Master here and Song Ryong only visits once a week (or less) for *dokusan* and *teisho* (often less than that).

Do you have a strong practice at Providence or Cambridge or is it weak and relaxed with many interruptions? For sixteen months now there has been, at this center, practically no practice and constant interruptions—now it is time for a stronger practice.

In any event, please write soon.

Ed

January 16, 1975

Dear Ed,

Thank you for your letter. It was very, very long. This is good. But I told you that opening your mouth is wrong. Only keep your mouth closed. You already understand. In the Heart Sutra it says, ". . . perceives that all five skandhas are empty and is saved from all suffering and distress." If you truly understand this, then in your mind there will be no places, no friends, no temples, no teachers. What is most important is how you keep your mind. Where you live is not important, if you keep your mind correctly. When you became a monk, you had beginner's mind. Now I think that you have lost this beginner's mind. I hope you will return to it soon.

In your letter you said that you "create the world around you" and that "each person creates his own heaven and hell." Words are very easy. Zen means not making all these things. Then there is nothing. This is true emptiness. True emptiness means no hindrance. Why do you make "world," "me," "other people," etc.? First you must understand your true self. Then you will be able to understand other people's minds. How can you teach other people if you don't understand yourself?

You say that other people won't listen to you. But what do you understand? What do you say? Do they want to hear your words? Do they want your understanding? Since you have your opinion and other people have theirs, there are differences, and people won't listen to you. First you must throw away all your opinions, all your cognition, your concern about your situation, and your explanations. Then there will be nothing. And then you will understand other people's minds. Your mind will be like a clear mirror. Red comes and it becomes red; white comes and it becomes white. When your mind is clear, then it is a reflection of other people's minds. If they are sad, then you are sad; if they are silent, you are silent; if they have desires, then you understand these desires. Then it is possible to teach others and to fix their minds.

Good and bad both are your true teachers. If you cut off your "small I," then there is no like or dislike, no good or bad. All things in the universe are your good friends and teachers. So you must kill your self. Then you will get freedom and you will have no hindrance. This is how you will find your true way. If you understand this true way, then only go and watch your step. Don't be attached to what is on the side of the road. Just go straight ahead.

Buddha once said, "If one mind is clear, then the whole universe is clear." If your mind cuts off all thinking and becomes clear, then your place, wherever it is, is clear. Don't worry about other people. If you have a strong practice, they will all follow you. Your mind is very strong; but your "self" is attached to your strong mind, so you have strong likes and dislikes, strong anger, frustration, bad thoughts about other people, and so on. You must completely cut off this strong mind, this strong I. This is very important. When you talk about your understanding, this is being attached to your mind. CUT OFF THIS I!

Somebody once asked Zen Master Jo-ju, "Does a dog have Buddha-nature?" Jo-ju answered, "No!" Do you understand this "No"? What does it mean? If you open your mouth, I will hit you thirty times. If you don't open your mouth, I will still hit you thirty times. What can you do? Thinking is no good, so put it all down.

You want to find a great Zen Master, or a place with hard training, or do a 100-day retreat, or come to Providence. If you don't let go of your mind, then none of these things can help you. You must understand what sitting Zen is. What is *sitting*? Sitting means cutting off all thinking and keeping not-moving mind. What is *Zen*? Zen means becoming clear. You are attached to the outside of Zen; you don't understand true Zen. If you really understand Zen, then it is not necessary to have a Zen Master, or a 100-day retreat, or a hard training place, or the Providence or Cambridge Zen Centers. Then you can do walking, standing, sitting, sleeping, talking, being silent—all these things will be your practice. Always keep a clear mind. Always return to your true self. Then there are no eyes, no ears, no nose, no tongue, no body, no mind, no color, no sound, no smell, no taste, no touch, no object of mind. Then you will understand "no attainment, with nothing to attain." You must cut off the "I want enlightenment" mind.

It is very important for you to fix your mind. The more you want enlightenment, the further away it will be. If you want to find a good place to practice Zen, no place you find will be good enough. But if you cut off all thinking and return to beginner's mind, that itself will be enlightenment. If you keep true empty mind, then any place you are is Nirvana. So you must very strongly keep a closed mouth, and you must learn from the blue sky, the white clouds, the deep quiet mountains, and the noisy cities. They are all just like this. That is your true great teacher. I hope you first kill your strong self and find clear mind all the time, then save all people from suffering.

> The blue mountains and green forests
> are the Patriarchs' clear face.
> Do you understand this face?
> A quarter is twenty-five cents.

See you later.
S. S.

March 8, 1975

Dear Soen-sa-nim,

How is it in Providence? Here it is beautiful—cool and rainy—very rare. I plan to leave here approximately July 15, and then return East to visit my mother, and you.

I have an open-my-mouth question:

Why is there all the practice with effort, if it is an effortless state we end at? Why sitting, *kong-ans,* chanting, etc? In my sitting, for the last ten to twelve months, there has been no (or little) difference between sitting and not sitting, only clarity. That is, my *kong-an* sitting is the same as sitting doing nothing (*shikantaza*), and making effort is the same as no effort. Making effort leads to a direction, at the beginning opposite to the later state of no-effort; later it becomes no-effort, so why spend three to five years making effort when it leads to no effort? Why not start with no effort, just being mindful as in the Hinayana Vipassana method or as with Krishnamurti? Why spend three to five years going away from no effort only to return?

Also, the Japanese Soto and Rinzai seem to put much more emphasis on effort—hard sitting, endless work, etc.— than you do. You put less emphasis on sitting and effort in practice. Why?

Also, you say *kensho,* enlightenment, is "clear mind." Maezumi and Hearn both disagree. From my own experience, I've experienced many times during the last four years states beyond clarity; states where "I" (mind and body) disappear and there is only the world seen, experienced with no separation, no space, no time, just this.

Is the latter state what you mean by "clear mind"?

If my sitting goes well, this state of oneness, of "like this," occurs every few days; if it goes badly, it does not occur often at all. But now, I see there is no difference between good sitting and bad sitting, between clarity and crowded, anxious mind.

But is there any point in training that one may be called enlightened? I think not. All is enlightenment, is it not?

Also, why is it that it takes twenty to thirty years to complete training under a Japanese Roshi, but much less under a Korean? What is it about the Japanese method that takes so long? Are they more thorough and complete? better or worse, or why?

You asked me: "What do I understand?"

I understand that there is nothing to understand, nothing to be done or to be practiced, only clear mind. But no one wants to hear this, they want to drink, dance, make noise, have opinions, and endlessly talk about love and compassion, which is only their idea of love and compassion.

I have little interest in becoming a teacher, very few listen anyway, and even when you talk at all, you are not being a good teacher most of the time.

So my teaching is to tell other people not to worry about the millions of different practices that one can do, only to sit. The method is not important; just sit, *kong-an, shikantaza,* breath counting. Then the real "I" functions with no thinking, no talking; then, sometimes, without knowing when, God or Buddha comes, like this, Reality.

Nor am I interested in attaining enlightenment. Enlightenment is only a word; either I have it now, or it will come of its own accord as long as I practice. What difference does it make?

But I am interested in how to show others that thinking, ideas, etc., are a blockage to clarity, at least in the beginning; to drop their opinions and emotions by whatever way they can.

Hope to see you in July or early August.

Sincerely,
Ed

P.S. By profession and training, I am an economist and planner. Until one or two years ago I was greatly optimistic about the *future* of the world in terms of food and war, etc., but knew it didn't matter because the world was too complicated to understand in ideas what was happening, let alone with sufficient accuracy to make any significant plans. But now I know, from a deep investigation of what is going on, that the world is in deep trouble, far more so than ever before, and perhaps too late in that trouble to do anything about it.

What really must be done is to revolutionize men's minds. But it is not now merely a matter of being a good teacher. Many, many people must experience this revolution now, or all the world could die. If it does, it does; but just as a good doctor will treat all diseases as they arise, then those who are able now must treat the diseases of mind—but quickly. There is no grace period of a hundred or a thousand years left—but perhaps only two or three decades more before the world falls apart and there is unbelievable suffering. And when I see suffering, I suffer. This suffering *must* be stopped.

March 22, 1975

Dear Ed,

Thank you for your letter. I will be glad to see you when you come to the East Coast.

In your letter, you talk a lot about effort and no effort. Put it all down. Why so much thinking? Why are you so attached to words? An eminent teacher said, "The ten thousand questions are one question. If you cut through the one question, then the ten thousand questions all disappear."

What do you want? If one person makes great effort, if another person makes no effort—don't worry. All that you need be concerned about is your own job. First finish your own great work; then you will understand everything. Sitting, walking, talking, laughing, eating—all is Zen. You must understand this.

Sitting is important. But true sitting doesn't depend on whether or not the body is sitting. You already know the story about Ma-jo doing hard sitting and Nam Ak picking up the tile and polishing it.

You say that I say enlightenment is clear mind. What is clear mind? Clear mind is only a name. Enlightenment is also only a name. If you say clear mind, it is not clear mind. If you say enlightenment, it is not enlightenment. Red is red; white is white. Only like this. This is clear mind; this is enlightenment. It is nothing at all. If you say that clear mind is enlightenment, I will hit you thirty times. If you say that clear mind is not enlightenment, I will still hit you thirty times. Don't be attached to clear mind or to enlightenment. Don't be attached to Zen words. You must be very careful. Zen Masters use their tongues to trap their students.

You say that when your sitting is good, a state of oneness beyond clarity occurs. What is oneness? What is good sitting or bad sitting? You must not check your mind. Checking your mind is a very bad Zen sickness. As fine as your speech is, it is only thinking. Give me one sentence before thinking.

You ask why it takes twenty or thirty years to complete training under a Japanese Zen Master. Under a Korean Zen Master, it takes infinite time. You go around comparing Japanese and Korean Zen and other kinds of Buddhism. This is your bad karma. Such things are simply not important! Put it down!

You say that you understand there is nothing to understand. But you understand enlightenment, emptiness, everything. Yet you haven't *attained* enlightenment or emptiness or everything. Understanding is thinking. Attainment is before thinking. If you open your mouth, you are wrong. I have already told you that you must keep your mouth closed. You must keep this rule!

The Third Patriarch said,

> The Great Way is not difficult
> for those who do not discriminate.
> Throw away likes and dislikes
> and everything will become clear.

Throw away teaching, throw away everything. If you say you are not attached to methods of practice, this is being attached to method. If you cut off your attachment, then your words ("the real 'I' functions without thinking or talking") are not necessary. You say, "sometimes, without knowing when, God or Buddha comes, like this, Reality." When Buddha comes, you must kill Buddha; when God comes, you must kill God. How is Buddha or God necessary? An eminent teacher said, "I go around the six realms of existence without asking for a drop of help from Buddhas or Bodhisattvas." Another eminent teacher said, "If I kill my parents, I can repent to Buddha. But if I kill Buddha, where can I repent?" You must understand this place of true repentance.

You say, "I am not interested in attaining enlightenment." But you are very interested; you are very attached to enlightenment. Why do you keep saying enlightenment, enlightenment, enlightenment? What is enlightenment? You must read the Heart Sutra. If you understand the true meaning of the Heart Sutra, then you will understand your true way.

Your teaching other people is like one blind man leading other blind men into a ditch. You must open your eyes. This is very necessary.

You think that the whole world is suffering, and you are afraid that the world will be destroyed. You want to save all people from suffering. So you are a great Bodhisattva, a great man. But a truly great man has no words or speech—only action. I want a short letter from you next time. You must go outside and ask the tree in front of the temple what the true way is. Then this tree will teach you. Don't write me anything else. Just tell me what the tree said to you.

Yours sincerely,
S. S.

80. Who Makes One?

One evening, after a Dharma talk at the Boston Dharmadhatu, a student asked Seung Sahn Soen-sa, "If everything is one, what's two?"

Soen-sa said, "Who makes everything one?"

"You do."

"I don't make one. *You* make one."

"Then why do you call it one?"

Soen-sa said, "You have an attachment to words." There were a few moments of silence. "Okay, I ask you: before you were born, were you zero or one?"

"Neither."

"Not zero?! Before you were born, this body didn't exist. So you were zero, okay?"

"Not zero."

Soen-sa said, "Not zero? This body *did* exist?" Then, pointing to the man's long blond hair, "Okay—before you were born, did you have this hair?"

The student hesitated a moment, then said, "No."

Soen-sa said, "Okay. Now your hair is one. After you die, will you have hair?"

"No."

"So this is for your hair, only your hair. Before you were born, your hair was zero. Now it is one. In the future, it will be zero. Okay?"

"Okay."

"This is the truth. So zero equals one, one equals zero. Okay?"

"Okay."

"So one times zero equals zero. Two times ten equals zero. Three times one hundred equals zero. Okay?"

"Ummm. . . . If you say so."

"You say one, you say two, you say three, you say many, many: all equals zero. So if you want one, you have one. If you want two, you have two. If you want one hundred, you have one hundred. Descartes said, 'I think, therefore I am.' If I think one, I have one. Before, you thought one, so you had one. I wasn't thinking one, so I didn't have one. So *you* say one; I don't say one."

"Then why don't you say that everything's zero?"

"Not zero." (Laughter from the audience.) " *You* say zero; I don't say zero."

"You say one."

"I say zero." (Loud, sustained laughter.) "You say one, I

185

say zero. You are attached to my words. I am not attached to words; I am free. Sometimes I say zero, sometimes not zero. So if you think one, you have one. If you think one hundred, you have one hundred. If you cut off all thinking, all is empty. If you think God, you have God. If you think Buddha, you have Buddha. If you are not thinking, there is no Buddha, no God. That is what the Buddha meant when he said, 'The whole universe is created by your thinking.' "

81. What Is *Your* Star?

Soon after Chung Gang attained enlightenment at the age of twenty-two, he went to see Zen Master Mang Gong. Mang Gong said to him, "Buddha became enlightened upon seeing the morning star in the eastern sky. But there are many stars. What is *your* star?"

Chung Gang dropped to his hands and knees and began feeling around on the floor.

Mang Gong said, "Ah, you have truly become a Buddha," and gave him Transmission.

82. The Story of Sul

Among the students of the great Zen Master Ma-jo, there was a layman named Chang. This man was a very devout Buddhist, who bowed and chanted sutras twice a day and paid frequent visits to the Zen Master. He would always take along his little daughter Sul.

The little girl was even more devout than her father. She would join him every day for bowing and chanting, and looked forward with the greatest pleasure to seeing the Zen Master. One day, during a visit, Ma-jo said to her, "Since you are such a good girl, I will give you a present. My present is the words *Kwanseum Bosal*. You must repeat the Bodhisattva's name over and over, as much as you can. Then you will find great happiness."

After they came home, Sul's father gave her a picture of the Bodhisattva to hang up on her wall. She spent many hours in front of it, chanting *Kwanseum Bosal, Kwanseum Bosal.* Gradually she came to chant all day long, wherever she was—while she was sewing, while she washing clothes, cooking, eating, playing, even while she was sleeping. Her parents were very proud of her.

Several years passed, and her friends had long since concluded that Sul was a little crazy. This didn't affect her at all; she continued to chant all day long, wherever she was. One day she was washing clothes in the river, beating the dirt out of them with a stick. Suddenly the great bell from Ma-jo's temple rang. The sound of the stick and the sound of the bell became one, and her mind opened. She was overwhelmed with joy; she felt as if the whole universe were dancing along with Kwanseum Bosal, who was none other than herself. She herself was Kwanseum Bosal! And Kwanseum Bosal was the earth, the sky, the great bell from Ma-jo's temple, the dirty clothes which lay in a heap on the riverbank. She ran back home, leaping for joy, and never chanted *Kwanseum Bosal* again.

During the next few days, her parents noticed a great change in her. Whereas before, she had been a quiet, well-behaved little girl, now she would burst into wild laughter for no reason, have long conversations with trees or clouds, run down the road to the village at breakneck speed, like a boy. Her father became so worried that he decided to peep in at her through the keyhole of her door to see what she was doing alone in her room. He looked in, and first saw the picture of Kwanseum Bosal on the wall, and next to it her altar, where the holy Lotus Sutra should have been, sur-rounded by incense and flowers. But today it wasn't there. Then he saw Sul, sitting in a corner, face to the wall, sitting on . . . the Lotus Sutra! He could hardly believe his eyes. After a moment of shock, he burst into the room, shouting. "What do you think you're doing! are you out of your mind! this is the holy scripture! why are you sitting on it!"

Sul smiled and said, calmly, "Father, what is holy about it?"

"It is Buddha's own words, it contains the greatest truths of Buddhism!"

"Can the truth be contained in language?"

At this, Chang began to realize that what had happened to his daughter was beyond his grasp. His anger turned to intense puzzlement.

"Then where do you think the truth is?"

"If I tried to explain," Sul said, "you wouldn't under-stand. Go ask Ma-jo and see what he says."

So Chang went and told Ma-jo the story of the past few days. After he had finished, he said, "Please, Master, tell me: is my daughter crazy?"

Ma-jo said, "Your daughter isn't crazy. *You* are crazy."

"What should I do?"

"Don't worry," Ma-jo said, and handed him a large rice-paper calligraphy, with the following inscription:

When you hear the wooden chicken crow in the evening,
you will know the country where your mind was born.
Outside my house, in the garden,
the willow is green, the flower is red.

"Just put this up in your daughter's room and see what happens."

Chang was now more confused than ever. He walked home like a man who has lost his direction. He could understand nothing.

When Sul read the calligraphy on her wall, she simply nodded and said to herself, "Oh, a Zen Master is also like this." Then she put the Lotus Sutra back on her altar, surrounded by incense and flowers.

After more hard training, she went to see Ma-jo at his temple. Zen Master Ho Am happened to be visiting Ma-jo at the time, and the two Masters invited Sul to sit down and join them for tea. After she had sat down and poured herself a cup of tea, Ho Am said to Ma-jo, "I hear that this young lady has been practicing very hard." Ma-jo said nothing. Ho Am turned to Sul and said, "I am going to test your mind."

"All right."

"In the sutra it says, 'The great Mount Sumeru fits into a mustard seed; someone enters and breaks the rocks to smithereens.' What does this mean?"

Sul picked up her cup and threw it against the wall, where it smashed.

Ma-jo laughed and clapped his hands. "Very good! Very good! Now *I* will test your mind."

"All right."

"In Buddhism, the word 'karma' is used very often. You have good Buddhist karma. So I ask you: what is karma?"

Sul said, "Excuse me, but could you explain the question once more, please?"

"In all the three vehicles of Buddhism, the concept of karma is used in one sense or another. I am asking you what precisely karma means."

Sul bowed to Ma-jo, said "Thank you," and then was silent.

Ma-jo smiled and said, "A very good trick. You understand."

As Sul grew up, she always kept a perfectly clear mind. Outside, her actions were ordinary actions; inside, her mind was the mind of a Bodhisattva. Eventually she married and raised a large, happy family, all of whom were devout Buddhists. Many people came to her for help and teaching. She became known as a great Zen Master.

One day,when she was an old woman, her granddaughter died. She cried bitterly during the funeral and kept crying back at her home, as the visitors filed past to offer their condolences. Everyone was shocked. Soon they were whispering. Finally one of them went up to her and said, "You have attained the great enlightenment, you already understand that there is neither death nor life. Why are you crying? Why is your granddaughter a hindrance to your clear mind?"

Sul immediately stopped crying and said, "Do you understand how important my tears are? They are greater than all the sutras, all the words of the Patriarchs, and all possible ceremonies. When my granddaughter hears me crying, she will enter Nirvana." Then she shouted to all the visitors, "Do you understand this?"

No one understood.

83. Dialogue with Swami X

One day a prominent yogi invited Seung Sahn Soen-sa to come talk with him during his stay in Cambridge. There were several dozen students present, and a large pile of fruits, which had been brought as presents, in front of the swami, who was sitting in a chair on a small podium. Soen-sa was offered a seat on the floor to his left.

After Soen-sa and three of his students who had come with him sat down, the swami offered him a piece of candy. One of Soen-sa's students said, "No, thank you," and explained that Soen-sa has diabetes.

The swami said, "Oh, that's too bad. Every day you should walk two miles. That is sure to help."

Soen-sa said, "Diabetes is very good. Form is emptiness, emptiness is form. This body is already emptiness. So my diabetes is emptiness. So it is very good."

The swami was silent for a few moments, then said, "Let us talk. Say something."

Soen-sa said, "How should you keep your mind during yoga?"

"We should merge with mind into the inner self. And the mind should be without any objects. Have you read Patanjali on yoga?"

"Then my self and my mind—are they the same or different?"

"When mind goes within, into the inner self, it becomes

one with the inner self. But when it comes out, for that time it is separate."

"Mind has no inside or outside. So how can it become one with the self or separate from it?"

"Then who acts outside, if not mind?"

"What is mind?"

The swami said, "Mind is the tendency of the self which goes out to do actions. When it goes inside, it becomes the self, and when it is outside, it does things in the world. The mind is no separate entity, it is not a modification of anything, it is nothing but the consciousness. When the universal consciousness becomes contracted and takes the form of outside objects, then we call it mind. And when the same mind goes inside and becomes the self, again it becomes the consciousness itself. It contracts and it expands."

Soen-sa said, "Mind has no inside and no outside. Thinking makes inside, outside, consciousness, mind—everything is made by thinking. So mind is no mind."

The swami said, "When mind takes the form of outside objects it becomes the mind. But when it goes inside and forgets all objects, it again becomes the self and the consciousness."

Soen-sa said, "Who makes inside, who makes outside, who makes consciousness, who makes objects?"

"Do you know who made *you?*"

"If you ask me, I will answer you."

"What do you think? Who made the world?"

Soen-sa said, "In front of you, there are many apples and oranges."

At this point, the Hindi translator, looking very confused, asked Soen-sa to repeat his answer. Then, knitting her brows, she relayed it to the swami.

The swami was silent for a few moments. Then he said, "Is that an answer?"

Soen-sa said, "Do you want another answer?"

"Yes."

"One plus two equals three."

"And suppose you take two from three, then . . .?"

"Only one."

"Suppose we take away that one also."

Soen-sa said, "Then I will hit you!"

The translator caught her breath. She was visibly shocked, and obviously didn't want to translate this last statement. But after a few moments, she did.

The swami looked extremely displeased. He jiggled his foot and said, "These answers don't make any sense. What knowledge do you have?"

Soen-sa said, "Okay, I will explain. I ask you now: one plus two equals three; one plus two equals zero—which one is correct?"

The swami said, "Everything is momentary change, you see. Sometimes it can be ten, or it can be five. It can be seven, it can be nine. It goes on changing. So there is nothing fixed. Everything is a momentary truth."

Soen-sa said, "If you say that everything changes, then you are attached to form."

The swami said, "I'm *not* attached to form! But *you* are attached to your questions and answers!"

Soen-sa laughed and said, "Yah, *that* is a good answer."

The swami said, "Why should one be attached to things that are always changing? Why should one desire them?"

"Okay, let me ask you . . ."

"No, *I* have a question for *you*. What is the purpose of our meeting together to talk about spiritual things?"

Soen-sa said, "Today is Saturday."

"This is not the answer of a philosopher! It is only the answer of a child!"

"Yes."

"In everything there is always some purpose, from the point of view of worldly life. For example, this man" (pointing to a devotee) "is here, and if I ask him, 'Why have you come here?', he will tell me, 'I have come to see you' or 'I have come to ask you something.' And answers should be such that people can understand them. So a person asks me questions if he has doubts, and getting an answer will remove his doubts. But your answers have no meaning and no purpose. It is just like a child playing."

Soen-sa said, "These other answers are children's answers. 'I came to see you'—all children understand this. But 'today is Saturday'—children do not understand this answer. So *your* answers are a child's answers."

The swami said, "Only if people understand what we say, only then does it have some meaning and some purpose. If nobody understands you, then what's the use of your questions and answers? Some meaning should come out of them."

Soen-sa said, "I understand that you are a great man. But you don't understand. So you are a child."

The swami said, "There is no question of great or small. But when we talk, we should use words and sentences in such a way that in our daily life, in worldly dealings, they will have some meaning. It must be explicit, from big to small. Both children and grownups should be able to understand them."

Soen-sa said, "Let me ask you one more question." Then, picking up an apple, "This is an apple, okay? But if you say that it is an apple, you have an attachment to name and form. And if you say that it is not an apple, you have an attachment to emptiness. Is this an apple or not?"

"Both."

"Both? I will hit you sixty times! To answer 'apple' is wrong; to answer 'not apple' is also wrong; to answer 'both' is doubly wrong. Why? This apple is made by thinking. It does not say, 'I am an apple.' People call it an apple. So it is made by thinking."

The swami said, "We understand that this grows on a tree."

Soen-sa said, "Yes! *That* is a good answer. A very good answer would be . . ." and bit into the apple.

The swami said, "Even without eating it, I can understand what this apple is. Those who don't understand need to eat it. You understood it by eating it. I understood it by just looking at it."

"Then a good answer would have been to hand it to me and say, 'Please eat.' "

"That's not necessary. I can see what it is."

"That is true. All words are not necessary."

The swami said, "There are many kinds of understanding. Eating isn't the only way. There is another way of understanding. For the time being, leave your philosophy and go to the market. Suppose you go and tell the shopkeeper about the apple and what it is, what size it is, and so on. He won't hand it to you to eat. In your daily life, this philosophy of yours is useless. One's philosophy should be practical. We should be able to apply it in our daily life. Our philosophy and our daily life should not be separate; they should be one. Philosophy should be such that ordinary people are able to use it. Today the world is such that the scientists won't believe such things. They won't believe anything that doesn't work."

Soen-sa said, "I am not a philosopher. I am not a scientist. I am not a Buddhist."

"Then what is your purpose?"

"You already understand."

The swami looked at his watch and said, "I must go now. We will talk later. It's not difficult to talk to you." Then, laughing, he said, "Since you are not a philosopher, I will give you an apple," and handed Soen-sa an apple.

Soen-sa handed it back and, smiling, said, "I will give it to you."

The swami said, "I am happy both ways, either to give or to receive."

Soen-sa said, "Thank you very much."

84. Big Mistake

One Sunday evening, after a Dharma talk at the International Zen Center of New York, a student asked Seung Sahn Soen-sa, "Does Big I ever make a mistake?"

Soen-sa said, "A big mistake."

The student said, "Who sees the mistake?"

Soen-sa said, "It has already appeared."

85. Language-Route and Dharma-Route

February 10, 1975

Dear Soen-sa-nim,

Thank you very much for your letter. It helped clear the air, which was getting dusty with too much conceptual thought. Black ink on white paper—only like this. You asked me many questions but really only one. What happens after death. I don't know; before I was born I did but I forgot. Your homework is very tough. Here are my answers.

To the man who drops ashes on the Buddha, and "the mouse eats cat-food, but the cat-bowl is broken":

Ice, water, steam   —a boiling bathtub

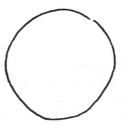

Legless cat scratches
Mouthless mouse eats
Broken bowl with no bottom
    or sides
When cat's food is swallowed
It does not move

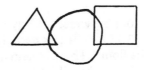

Your poem was wonderful.

Here is one for you:

Without special purpose
my life is complete
In the cave at midnight
there is still some light
But if the mind moves one inch
incense ash falls like thunder

197

KATZ
How much does it weigh?
You must bring the scales.

With a deep bow

Steve

February 23, 1975

Dear Steve,
How are you doing lately? Thank you for your letter. I
was waiting for it and was glad to receive it.
In your letter you said, "black ink on white paper—only
like this." These are very fine words. But there are two kinds
of "like this" answers: language-route and Dharma-route.
For example, take the following *kong-an*:

Here is a bell.
If you say it is a bell, you are attached to name and
form.
If you say it is not a bell, you are attached to empti-
ness.
Is this a bell or not?

I will show you four answers: 1. Only hit the floor. 2. "The
bell is laughing." 3. "Outside it is dark, inside it is light." Or,
"The bell is on the floor." These statements are only like this.
They are good answers, but they are not complete answers.
4. Pick up the bell and ring it. This is a 100% complete
answer. So it is possible to understand "like this" and yet not
give the best answer. Language-route answers are good, but
sometimes they are not complete. The Dharma-route answer
is the complete answer. When a question is wide, the language-route and the Dharma-route become one. So to the
question, "What is Buddha?", there are many complete answers: "Three pounds of flax," "Dry shit on a stick," "The
wall is white, the rug is blue," etc. But with a narrow question, the language-route and the Dharma-route are different.

So to the bell question, there is only one complete answer. The same is true for the mouse *kong-an.* The language-route is not complete; you must find the Dharma-route, then you will come up with a good answer. This answer is only one point.

You drew a triangle, circle, and square. If you are thinking, this is a demon's action. If you cut off all thinking, everything is the truth. So if you cut off all thinking, these figures are not necessary. Shit is Buddha, vomit is Buddha— they are the truth, they are just like this. If you keep a discriminating mind, why stop at three figures? More are possible, and the figures you could draw are endless. These are only devices for teaching Zen; they do not really exist. You must not be attached to form. You must finish your homework. This is very important. You must understand that a quarter is twenty-five cents.

Your poem is very good. But what does "my life is complete" mean? If you use "complete," you must take out "my life." If you use "my life," you must take out "complete." How can you hear "the sound of incense ash falling like thunder"? You wrote, "KATZ" and "How much does it weigh?" I already asked you how much it weighs. If you want to understand this weight, you need a scale without measurements.

Here is a poem for you:

The snowman Bodhidharma sweats and grows
    smaller, smaller.
The sound of his heartbeat shatters heaven and hell.
His eyebrows drop off, then his eyes, then his
    carrot nose.
A little boy shouts, "Bodhidharma is dying!"

Sincerely yours,
S.S.

86. The Tathagata

One Thursday evening, after a Dharma talk at the Cambridge Zen Center, a student said to Seung Sahn Soen-sa, "I have a very technical question. Would you discourse on the concept of the Tathagata?"

Soen-sa said, "In America, people sign checks and documents. But in the Orient, people use a rubber stamp or seal. The Tathagata is only this. There are three kinds of Zen: Theoretical Zen, Tathagata Zen, and Patriarchal Zen. Theoretical Zen is like stamping a piece of paper: anyone can understand the sign. Tathagata Zen is like stamping water: people can only hear the sound; the stamp disappears immediately. Patriarchal Zen is like stamping space: no one can understand. Things come and they go, without hindrance. With water, there is a little hindrance. With paper, there is attachment. So Tathagata is the middle of these three. 'Form is emptiness, emptiness is form' means 'no form, no emptiness.' If you want to understand the true meaning of the Tathagata, listen to this *kong-an*: Somebody once asked Zen Master Jo-ju, 'What is Buddha?' Jo-ju said, 'Go drink tea.' This person had been sitting Zen for a while, so he understood a little. He shouted 'KATZ!!!' Then Jo-ju said, 'Did you drink tea?' What does this dialogue mean? If you understand it, then you understand the true meaning of Tathagata."

"I think I understand."

Soen-sa said, "If you are thinking, you don't understand.

'No form, no emptiness' is before thinking. If you are thinking, this is not Tathagata Zen."

A second student said, "What does the dialogue mean?"

Soen-sa said, "I hit you thirty times." (Laughter from the
audience).

"But I don't understand the story."

"I already explained: I hit you thirty times."

"Oh, now I understand."

"What do you understand?" (Laughter.)

"Ouch!"

Soen-sa said, "Did you have supper?"

"No."

"You must be hungry. Go have something to eat."

The student bowed.

87. Bodhidharma and I

Once Seung Sahn Soen-sa and a student of his attended a
talk at a Zen center in California. The Dharma teacher spoke
about Bodhidharma. After the talk, someone asked him
"What's the difference between Bodhidharma's sitting in
Sorim for nine years and your sitting here now?"

The Dharma teacher said, "About five thousand miles."

The questioner said, "Is that all?"

The Dharma teacher said, "Give or take a few miles."

Later on, Soen-sa asked his student, "What do you think
of these answers?"

"Not bad, not good. But the dog runs after the bone."

"How would *you* answer?"

"I'd say, 'Why do you make a difference?' "

Soen-sa said, "Not bad. Now *you* ask *me*."

"What's the difference between Bodhidharma's sitting in Sorim for nine years and your sitting here now?"

"Don't you know?"

"I'm listening."

"Bodhidharma sat in Sorim for nine years. I am sitting here now."

The student smiled.

88. Correspondence with an Ordained American Lawyer

December 26, 1974

Dear Soen-sa-nim,

Thank you for the letter, the instructions, and the poem. This must be a short letter, because I have a great deal of office work to do. I still haven't found the answer to your mouse kong-an.

As for practice, we continue to sit each morning, but that is only Bodhisattva practice—like bowing. The main practice comes during the times when I must deal with people and responsibilities during the day. I try to respond appropriately to each thing that occurs and at the same time to watch carefully for any wish or feeling that something should be different than it is. When such a feeling comes, I swing my ax.

Thank you for your very helpful letters and for all your teaching. I will write again about my homework when I get a chance.

Hapchang,
An Hanh

January 2, 1975

Dear Ven. An Hanh,

Happy New Year! I hope you soon finish your homework, attain enlightenment, and save all people from suffering.

I told you before that a quarter is twenty-five cents. If you understand the true meaning of this, then you will understand the mouse kong-an. For example, somebody comes and asks me for twenty-five cents. I give him a quarter. But he shouts to me, "This is not twenty-five cents; this is a quarter!" I say, "Yah, this is twenty-five cents." But he doesn't believe me. "No no, this is a quarter, not twenty-five cents!" This goes on for a while. So finally I take out two dimes and a nickel and give them to him. He is very happy. This man only understands twenty-five cents, he doesn't understand what a quarter is. So go back and check the *kong-an*. You only understand mouse, cat-food, cat-bowl, and broken. You don't understand the meaning behind them. You must find this behind-meaning. The meaning behind the quarter is twenty-five cents; the meaning behind twenty-five cents is the quarter. You are already a great man. Why are you attached to outside words? The apple is red. But the apple is sweet. Don't touch the color; you must taste sweet. Name and form are not necessary. Only eat.

Here is another poem for you:

> The moon is white, the snow is white,
>   all the ground is white.
> The mountain is deep, the night is deep,
>   the guest mind is deep.
> The owl calls "Too-whoo"; the echo is very cold.
> He doesn't know that light from the full moon
>   covers the fifteenth day.

I will wait for your homework. Please send me a good answer.

You say that your sitting is not your main practice. This is no good. To think in terms of main practice and not main practice—this is divided mind. What is main practice? An eminent teacher said, "Sitting, lying down, talking, silence, moving—in all these you must become one mind." This one mind is no mind. No mind is true empty mind. True empty mind is before thinking. Before thinking is only like this. Then where is main practice and not main practice? When sitting, only sit; when talking, only talk; when working, only work. All are your main practice. Sometimes desires appear. This is not good and not bad. Only keep clear mind. You must not touch, you must not swing your ax. An eminent teacher said, "I wander around the six realms and never ask Buddhas or Bodhisattvas for the least bit of help." Thinking is good. The mind that swings the ax is also thinking. So don't worry. But you must keep everything as your main practice. I hope that you find main practice in all things, that all your actions are one-mind actions and that you save all people.

See you later.
S. S.

January 7, 1975

Dear Soen-sa-nim,
    Re the mouse *kong-an:*

> I was never born.
> I will never die.
> Right now I am being born.
> Right now I am dying.
> $0 = \infty$

To say this is correct would be to be attached to name and form. To say it is wrong would be to not know why the cat-bowl is broken. What do you say?

Hapchang,
An Hanh

January 11, 1975

Dear An Hanh,

Thank you for your letter. Your answer to this *kong-an* is very good, but it is 84,000 miles away from the true answer.

I hit you thirty times!

Is this right or wrong?

I had a dream last night:

$$\infty = 0$$

Right now I am being born,
right now I am dying.
But I was never born,
I will never die.
No time, no space, no hindrance;
flying in the sky with absolute freedom.
How wonderful it is!
However, the bone of space appears abruptly
and crashes into my skull.
Aaiiieeee!!!.........I wake up.
Moonlight shines through the window onto
the floor.

Is this answer enough for you or not? If you say it is enough, then you will find the true meaning of why the cat-bowl is broken. If you say it is not enough, then you are still in this dream. You must wake up! I will give you the key to open this *kong-an*: The Biok An Lok (Blue Cliff Records) says, "When you see smoke from behind the mountain, you know there is fire. When you see horns above a stone wall, you know there is a cow behind it."

S. S.

January 31, 1975

Dear Soen-sa-nim,

Thank you for your last two letters. I am very glad to hear that you have gotten your permanent residence card and also that you will now be able to make a trip back to Korea.

Thank you also for the invitation to accompany you, but

I'm afraid that is not possible this year. There is much work to do in my office and with the College of Oriental Studies and no one else to attend to it if I go traveling. Perhaps next year or the year after I can visit Asia. If so, I hope you will give me some introductions to monks in Korea.

It would be wonderful if you are able to stop in Los Angeles on your way. If so, we would all look forward to seeing you.

My homework is stuck. You have been very kind in giving me directions about the mouse *kong-an,* but I am still unsure about it. Recently you wrote, "Moonlight shines through the window onto the floor. —Is this answer enough for you or not?" I think you are telling me to live with the "like this" aspect of it and not to chase freedom-mind. Yet before, you sent me poems saying that I should understand that four quarters make a dollar—which I took to mean that I should not cling to any of the various aspects of it—so I don't know. Maybe I am conceptualizing too much. Certainly I feel stuck.

You also wrote that the key to the mouse *kong-an* was in a statement by the Biok An Lok about the fire in the mountains and the cow behind the wall. You have told me before to see the meaning behind this *kong-an,* but I am still too stupid to know what you are driving at. The first part (the mouse part) points at 360°. That is plain. The bowl part points behind that? What is behind 360°???? I don't know.

Maybe it is the final throwing away of the idea of the Zen circle or of "like this" or of any special state of mind. So now mostly I just don't know and watch. However, this business requires that I give you an answer to the *kong-an,* "What is the meaning of 'the cat-bowl is broken'?" So here is my answer:

It's nothing special.

Finally, the Temple Rules you composed are really good for Americans. I will try to circulate them, because they get right at the business of playing games with other people's heads, which is a major fault of most of us. We all seem to have a lot of mouth-karma, and these will help to halt it.

See you,
An Hanh

February 12, 1975

Dear An Hanh,

Thank you for your letter. How are you doing lately? I hope you are keeping this "stuck" mind strongly and that you soon get enlightenment.

You and I have the same karma; neither one of us will be able to visit Korea this spring. I must stay because now I am the abbot of Won Gak Sa temple in New York City, and we are beginning the International Zen Center of New York. There are many Korean Buddhists who want me to spend time there, so now I have much work to do between Providence, Boston, and New York.

I like your "stuck" mind very much. Finding a good answer to the mouse *kong-an* is not as important as keeping this "stuck mind." Having this mind is your true treasure. But if you only keep it for yourself, then it becomes like any other desire. So you must share this treasure with others to help all people. This is why we use *kong-ans* and interviews, and why we must get enlightened.

Here is another hint for you.

$$3 \times 3 = 9$$
$$4 + 5 = 9$$
$$10 - 1 = 9$$
$$18 / 2 = 9$$

Here are many different examples, but behind each one is the same answer: 9. This *kong-an* is similar. It is a very good one because all the words—mouse, cat-food, bowl, and broken —all point to the same one thing. You must find this one thing. Before, I gave you many hints, and if you are not attached to my words you will see that they are not different from one another. They all point to this behind-meaning.

Your answer is not good or bad, it is nothing special. But "it is nothing special" has a very special meaning. The meaning behind this is "just like this."

You said in your letter that the Temple Rules are very good. Thank you very much. I am enclosing some new *kong-ans,* which I hope you will find useful.

See you later.
S. S.

April 7, 1975

Dear Soen-sa-nim,

I hear that your Zen centers are springing up on the East Coast like mushrooms after a Spring rain. That is wonderful. I am sure that many people will be helped toward awakening.

About my homework, "the cat-bowl is broken," there is nothing to say.

I have been looking for ways to talk to Americans about Zen, using language and examples that will seem familiar to them. One way that I have used the Dharma Speeches at the International Buddhist Meditation Center is something like the following: (Please let me know if you approve of this style of talking.)

"In college psychology classes there is an experiment they use to teach you about your perceptions. They take three pails of water: one with hot water, one with ice water, and one with the water at room temperature. The person doing the experiment puts his right hand into the hot water and at the same time puts his left hand into the ice water. He leaves them there thirty seconds or so to get used to the temperature. Then he takes both his hands at the same time and puts them into the third bucket—the one with room temperature water inside. That same water will feel cold to his right hand, which has been in the hot water, and warm to his left hand, which has been in the cold water. Try it. You'll see for yourself.

"What does that tell us about Zen? It shows that such dualistic categories as hot and cold depend on your having a particular viewpoint from which you are observing them. 'Cold' only means 'colder than my hand' and 'hot' only means 'hotter than my hand.' Without the reference point, 'my hand,' words like hot and cold have no meaning at all —they are nonsense.

"The same thing is true of all dualistic categories: hot and cold, light and dark, good and bad, being and non-being, etc.

"So that shows you what you learn by sitting Zen. You learn to relate without any such reference point. The 'I' gets eliminated as a particular point of view. Without the viewpoint of an 'I,' there are no such things as good and bad, being and non-being. All that kind of thinking becomes literally nonsense. Everything is just what it is without any relative qualities added. Red comes and it is red. Pain comes and it hurts. When the sun shines, the room becomes bright. Only like this.

"I only say these things to encourage you to sit Zen. These words have no Zen in them. Understanding is nothing. You must experience for yourself. Work hard and awaken. Then save all sentient beings."

Maybe this is too much talking, but people seem to like it and it seems to encourage them to sit Zen.

I have not heard from the Providence Zen Center since January. I hope they have not taken my name off their mailing list. I look forward to seeing you on your next trip to the West Coast.

Thank you for your teaching.

Sincerely,
An Hanh

April 17, 1975

Dear An Hanh,

Thank you for your letter and your kind words.

I have been waiting eagerly for the answer to your homework, but you said there is nothing to say. So I am very sad. This *kong-an* is too easy. All you need to understand is that a quarter is twenty-five cents. Only this.

Thank you very much for showing me how you teach. This teaching style is very good. But it is a little bit unclear. You say that relative qualities are nonsense and that everything is just what it is without any relative qualities added. But red, too, is relative. Pain is relative. Sun, shines, bright —all these are relative. You say that relative qualities are all nonsense. So why do you use them here? And if the "I" is eliminated as a particular point of view, how does red come? Who sees red? Who feels pain? Who understands "like this"?

There are three areas: the relative area, the nonsense area, and the "like this" area. In your teaching, from the relative area to the nonsense area is clear. But from nonsense to "like this" is not clear. People may have some difficulty understanding this.

An eminent teacher said, "To cure the sickness of deluded views, we must give people mirage medicine. When the sickness is cured, then we must take away the mirage medicine." How do we take away this mirage medicine? This is very important. If we don't take away the medicine, then the patient will fall down into the mirage.

In your teaching, you are trying to cure the sickness of attachment to opposites, and you use nonsense medicine. But how do you take away this nonsense medicine? Where does this nonsense go? So the area from nonsense to "like this" is not clear.

Here is an example of correct teaching: Cold and hot are made by thinking. If you cut off thinking, all opposites disappear. This is the Absolute. So there is no good and no bad, no dark and no light, no cold and no hot. But before thinking, there are no words and no speech. If you open your mouth, you are wrong. So to say "no cold and no hot" is also wrong. There is only KATZ, only HIT. But this itself is being attached to emptiness. So in true emptiness before thinking, you only keep a clear mind. All things are just as they are. It is like a clear mirror. Red comes and the mirror is red; white comes and the mirror is white. Cold comes: only cold; hot comes: only hot.

I hope this example is helpful. You must check where the medicine comes and where it is taken away.

I am also sending you a copy of the Dharma Speech that I will give at the opening ceremony of the International Zen Center of New York. How are your teaching and my teaching different? If you check this, then the Dharma Speech will teach you. It is very necessary first to cure the mind that separates the world into opposites. But when people understand "like this," that is also thinking, attachment to "like this." The Dharma Speech is really over when I say, "One two three four; five six seven eight." All the rest is explanation. But explanation is necessary. Then I once more check people's minds with a question about same or different. The final sentence means throwing everything away: same or different, explanations, "like this," Dharma Speeches, everything.

I am sorry about the newsletters. I will speak to the Providence Director and have him bring you up to date.

I hope I will see you soon.

Sincerely yours,
S.S.

89. Saving All People

One evening, after a Dharma talk at the Cambridge Zen Center, a student asked Seung Sahn Soen-sa, "When you say you are here to save all people, does that mean only to help them get enlightened or also to save them from hunger, war, and pain?"

Soen-sa said, "I have already finished saving all people."

There was a long silence.

"Do you understand what this means?"

Another long silence.

"Put it down. Okay?"

90. Dialogue at Tal Mah Sah

One Sunday, after a Dharma talk at Tal Mah Sah Temple in Los Angeles, Layman Bon Won came up to Seung Sahn Soen-sa and asked, "What is the realm of enlightenment?"

Soen-sa said, "Don't you know?"

Bon Won hit the floor.

Soen-sa said, "I don't believe you. Give me another answer."

"Outside it's very hot today."

Soen-sa said, "Good. Now let me ask you a question. Long ago, when Zen Master Se Sahn attained enlightenment, he wrote this stanza:

> When hair is white, mind is not white.
> Men have said this for a long time.
> Listen! a wooden chicken is crowing!
> Hear it and finish a great man's work.

What do these last two lines mean?"

"I ate lunch, so I'm not hungry now."

"I don't care about your lunch. Only *you* know whether your belly is full. I'm asking you about the wooden chicken crowing. What does that mean?"

"Cock-a-doodle-doo."

"Are you a wooden chicken?"

"Why are you playing a flute with no holes?"

Soen-sa said, "Even if you killed all the Buddhas, I wouldn't believe you. The meaning of 'a great man's work' is already in the poem. Which line contains this meaning?"

"There's a lot of smog in the Los Angeles sky."

"No good. Read the poem again."

Bon Won read the poem and said, "Have you had lunch?"

"No good. The meaning is in the poem. Read it again."

Bon Won read the poem once again and was silent.

Soen-sa said, "You still don't know. Now *you* ask *me.*"

"What does it mean to finish a great man's work?"

Soen-sa said, "When hair is white, mind is not white."

At this, Bon Won laughed loudly, and Soen-sa joined him.

91. The Boat Monk

Long ago, in China, the great Zen Master Yak Sahn had two chief disciples—Un Am and Dok Song. Both of them received Transmission from him and became Zen Masters themselves. Un Am was a powerfully-built, tireless man, with a voice like a great bronze bell and a laugh that made the ground shake. He soon became very famous as a teacher; many hundreds of disciples came to study with him. Dok Song, on the other hand, was a small, thin man, whose nature was so reserved that people rarely took notice of him. Only now and then he would say or do something that echoed in their minds for days afterwards.

When Master Yak Sahn died, Dok Song went to Un Am and said, "You are now a great Zen Master. You have many students, many temples. I approve of this. But my way is different. It leads to mountains, rivers, and clouds. After I have gone, please find one good student and send him to me, so that I can pay my debt to our Master."

With these words, Dok Song left for the province of Hwa Jong. There, he put aside his monk's clothing, let his hair grow, and bought a small boat, in which he would row people from one bank of the river to the other. So Dok Song lived the life of a simple ferryman, in perfect obscurity and freedom.

Many years passed. In the nearby province of Hon Am, there lived a young man named Son Hae. He had become a monk at the age of nine and had studied the sutras diligently since then, learning from all the foremost scholars in the area and mastering many volumes of Mahayana texts. Eventually, he acquired a reputation as one of the greatest Dharma teachers in the country, and people from all over came to hear his lectures and stay at his temple.

One day, after a particularly fine lecture, someone asked him, "Master, please explain to me—what is the Dharma body?"

"The Dharma body doesn't exist," said Son Hae.

The questioner continued, "And what is the Dharma eye?"

"The Dharma eye is without flaw."

Suddenly, from the back of the lecture hall, there was a burst of laughter, so powerful that it made the ground shake. Son Hae paused for a few moments in the shocked silence that followed, then descended from the podium and walked down the aisle to the back of the hall. He stopped in front of the old monk who had laughed, bowed once, and said, "Forgive me, Venerable Sir, but where is my mistake?"

The monk smiled, in deep appreciation of Son Hae's humility. "Your teaching is not incorrect," he said, "but you haven't even glimpsed the ultimate Dharma. What you need is the instruction of a keen-eyed Master."

"Won't you be kind enough to teach me?" Son Hae said.

"I'm sorry, but that's out of the question. Why don't you go to Hwa Jong province? There's a certain boatman there who will show you the way."

"A boatman? What kind of boatman can he be?"

"Above him," said the old monk, "there is no place for a roof; below him, there is no place for a pin. He may look like an ordinary boatman, but go speak to him. You'll see."

So Son Hae dismissed his many students, put aside his monk's clothing, and traveled to Hwa Jong.

After several days, Son Hae found the boatman. He turned out to be a skinny old man, shabbily dressed, who indeed looked like any other boatman and merely nodded as Son Hae stepped into the ferry. He rowed a few strokes, then let the boat drift and said, "Venerable Sir, what temple are you staying at?"

Son Hae recognized this innocent question as a challenge. He sat up, at attention, and said, "What is like it doesn't stay; what stays isn't like it."

"Then what can it be?" said Dok Song.

"Not what is before your eyes."

"Where did you learn this?"

"The eye can't see; the ear can't hear."

Up to this point, Son Hae had put up a decent fight. But the Master understood his mind perfectly, and when he suddenly shouted "KATZ!!!", Son Hae could find nothing to say. A few moments passed. Then the Master said, "Even the truest statement is a stake in the ground, which a donkey can be tethered to for ten thousand aeons."

Son Hae was by now thoroughly at a loss. His face turned white. He could hardly breathe.

Again the Master spoke. "I have let down a thousand feet of fishing line; the fish is just beyond the hook. Why don't you say something?"

Son Hae opened his mouth, but no words came out. Just then, the Master swung round his oar and hit him full on, with such force that he was hurled into the river. He fell down through the water, and when he came up, sputtering and gasping, he grabbed on to the side of the boat. As he was pulling himself up, the Master shouted, "Tell me! Tell me!"

and knocked him back into the river. But this time, as soon as Son Hae felt the sharp sting of the oar, his mind exploded, and he understood everything.

When he surfaced, he trod water and nodded three times. The Master beamed with pleasure, and, extending his oar, pulled him back into the boat. For a few minutes they sat looking at each other. Then the Master said, "You can play with the silken line at the end of the rod, but as long as you don't disturb the clear water, you will be doing well."

Son Hae said, "What are you trying to accomplish by letting down the fishing line?"

The Master said, "A hungry fish swallows bait and hook together. If you think in terms of existence or non-existence, you will be caught and cooked for dinner."

Son Hae laughed and said, "I don't understand a word you're saying. I can see your tongue flapping, but where is the sound?"

"I have been fishing in this river for many years," the Master said, "and only today have I caught a golden fish."

Son Hae clapped his hands over his ears.

"That's right. Just like this—how wonderful!" said the Master. "Now you are a free man. Wherever you go, you must leave no traces. In all the years that I spent studying with Master Yak Sahn, I learned nothing but that. Now you understand, and I have paid my debt."

All day and all night the two men drifted on the river, talking and not talking. When dawn came, they rowed to shore, and Son Hae stepped out of the boat. "Good-bye," said the Master. "You needn't think of me again. Everything else is unnecessary."

Son Hae walked away. After a while, he turned around for one last look. The Master waved at him from the middle of the river, then rocked back and forth until the boat capsized. Son Hae watched for the Master's head to surface, but it never did. He could only see the overturned boat slowly floating downstream and out of sight.

92. When the Bell Is Rung, Stand Up

One morning, during Yong Maeng Jong Jin at the Providence Zen Center, a student walked into the interview room and bowed to Seung Sahn Soen-sa. Soen-sa said, "Do you have any questions?"

The student said, "No."

Soen-sa said, "Then I will ask you a question. What is the true way?"

The student said, "Through the door into the kitchen."

Soen-sa said, "That is not the true way."

The student hit him.

Soen-sa said, "Aie, aie!"

The student leaned over and said, "Can I help you?"

Soen-sa said, "No. But I have another question for you. An eminent teacher once said, 'When the bell is rung, stand up; when the drum is hit, bow down.' What does this mean?"

The student said, "The bird flies in the sky."

Soen-sa said, "You are holding a stick and trying to hit the moon. Let me give you a hint. In our temple every morning and evening, after the bell chant the *moktak* master hits the *moktak*. What does everyone do then?"

"Stand up."

"And when the *moktak* is hit again, what do they do?"

"Bow down."

"We use the *moktak*; in China they use bells and drums. The signals are different; the actions are the same. So now you understand: 'When the bell is rung, stand up; when the drum is hit, bow down.' What does this mean?"

The student stood up and bowed to Soen-sa.

Soen-sa said, "That's right. Always keep this mind. This is your true way."

93. The Story of Mun Ik

There was once a great Zen Master named Poep An Mun Ik. He founded many temples, gave the Transmission to sixty-three of his disciples, and was the First Patriarch of the Poep An school of Zen.

When Mun Ik was a student under Zen Master Na Han, he was known for his phenomenal memory. He could recite many sutras word for word. He had also meditated a great deal, and his mind had become clear. He used to say to those who asked him about the truth, "All the three worlds, all Dharmas, and all Buddhas are made by the mind alone."

At this time in China, there were many wandering monks, who had freed themselves from all attachments and would travel from monastery to monastery and from Master to Master, like clouds across the empty sky. They were without hindrance.

Mun Ik had been admiring these monks and their way of life for some time. One day he decided to do as they did. He went to Na Han and said, "I've come to say goodbye, Master.

I'm going to live the life of no hindrance from now on. So tomorrow I'll be leaving you."

The Master raised his eyebrows a tiny bit and said, "Fine, if you think you're ready."

Mun Ik said, "Oh, I'm ready all right."

"Well," said the Master, "let me test you, just to make sure. You often say that the whole universe is made by the mind. Look over there in the garden. Do you see those large rocks?

"Yes."

"Tell me then—are they inside your mind or outside it?"

Without the slightest hesitation, Mun Ik answered, "Of course, they are inside my mind. How can there be anything outside it?"

The Master chuckled and said, "In that case, you'd better go get a good night's sleep. It's going to be heavy traveling tomorrow, with all those rocks inside your mind."

Mun Ik flushed with embarrassment and confusion, and looked down at the ground.

After a few moments, the Master said, "When you try to understand, you are like a man dreaming that he can see. The truth is right in front of you. It is alive, and infinitely great. How can human words contain it?"

Mun Ik bowed deeply and said, "Please, Master, teach me. I don't understand."

The Master said, "At this moment, you don't understand. This not-understanding is the earth, the sun, the stars, and the whole universe."

As soon as Mun Ik heard these words, his mind shot open. He bowed again and said, "Ah, Master, what else is ready now?"

Suddenly the Master shouted, "Mun Ik!"

Mun Ik shouted back, "Yes!"

"Very good," said the Master. "Now that you are ready, you may go."

94. What Did You Say?

One Thursday evening, after a Dharma talk at the Cambridge Zen Center, a student asked Seung Sahn Soen-sa, "What are you?"

Soen-sa said, "What did you say?"

The student said, "What are you?"

Soen-sa said, "What did you say?"

The student said, very slowly this time, "What . . . are . . . you?"

Soen-sa said, "Thank you very much." There was brief laughter in the audience, and then silence. Soen-sa said, "Do you understand?"

The student said, "No."

Soen-sa said, "I said, 'Thank you very much.' What are you?"

The student said, "I don't know."

Soen-sa said, "I hit you. Now do you understand?"

The student said, "No."

Soen-sa said, "Okay. You asked me, 'What are you.' I answered, 'What did you say?' You said again, 'What are you?' I answered again, 'What did you say?' You said one more time, 'What are you?' So I said, 'Thank you very much.' The dialogue was already finished. But you didn't know that. So I asked you, 'What are you?' You didn't know. So I hit you. Do you understand? 'What did you say?' was my answer to your question. Everybody understood this answer. So you were teaching everybody. So I said, 'Thank you very much.' But you didn't understand your own teaching. So I hit you."

The student sat for a few moments with an intensely puzzled expression on his face, then slowly bowed.

95. Much Ado About Nothing

Zen Master Ku Sahn wrote as follows to Ven. Dok Sahn, abbot of Sambosa Temple:

"Once Ang Sahn asked Zen Master Wi Sahn Yung-wu, 'Where does the true Buddha dwell?'

"Wi Sahn answered, 'When origination and matter come together, they become light. This light is emptiness, and this empty is full. When all phenomena are extinguished and return to the origin, then nature and form become clear. Origination is origination; matter is matter. Only like this: this is the true Buddha.'

"At these words, Ang Sahn was enlightened.

"Now, Dok Sahn, what is your view?"

Dok Sahn wrote in reply:

"It is said that the mind has no place of abode. Dok Sahn, the general of the guards who keep the gate of Sambosa on Robin Mountain, also has no place of abode and no view.

"Regarding the dialogue between Ang Sahn and Wi Sahn —I hit them both thirty times and give their bodies to a hungry dog."

Zen Master Ku Sahn wrote back:

"In your letter you said that you are the general of the guards who keep the gate of Sambosa. But in true emptiness, there is no entry and no exit. So what do you guard?

"You also said that you hit Ang Sahn and Wi Sahn thirty times. Please give me an answer that is before words. You hit them thirty times. Whom do you hit?"

Dok Sahn then wrote to Seung Sahn Soen-sa:

"How should I answer these questions? I look forward to your kind instruction."

Soen-sa answered Zen Master Ku Sahn:

"The sword of the general who keeps the gate at Robin Mountain kills Buddhas when it meets them and kills Patriarchs when it meets them. If Ku Sahn opens his mouth here, he too shall have no way to escape being killed by the pitiless sword.

"Regarding the second question—it is Ang Sahn and Wi Sahn who are hit. Why do you carry these thirty hits around on your own back?

"KATZ!!!

"The sky is blue, and the grass is green."

96. An Ambush in the Fields of Dharma

One morning, during Yong Maeng Jong Jin at the Providence Zen Center, a student walked into the interview room and bowed to Seung Sahn Soen-sa. Soen-sa said, "Do you have any questions?"

The student said, "Yes. A great Zen Master once asked his students, 'What is Buddha-nature?' One student shouted 'KATZ!!!' One student said, 'Take the horns of a rabbit and lift the moon out of the water.' One student said, 'The bee goes to the flower.' Which of these answers is the best?"

Soen-sa said, "They are all bad."

The student said, "Why?"

Soen-sa said, "The bee goes to the flower."

The student said, "That's a terrible answer."

Soen-sa said, "Why?"

The student said, "Outside the window, the tree is green."

Soen-sa said, "Ah, if you hadn't told me, I would have lost my way."

97. Un-Mun's Short-Answer Zen

One day a student asked Zen Master Un-mun, "What is it that passes over Buddha and all the eminent teachers?"

Un-mun answered, "Cake."

Another student asked him, "If you are not thinking, are there any mistakes?"

Un-mun answered, "Sumi Mountain."

Someone else asked him, "What is my original face?"

Un-mun said, "Sightseeing among mountains and rivers."

This was the way Un-mun taught Zen, always giving short answers to his students' questions. Often he would use only one word to point to the student's mind.

A student asked him, "What is the keenest sword?"

Un-mun answered, "Patriarch."

Another student asked him, "What is the true Dharma of Buddhism?"

Un-mun answered, "Wide."

Another student asked, "When does a chicken's egg hatch?"

Un-mun answered, "Echo."

Someone else said, "If I kill my parents, I can repent to Buddha. If I kill Buddha and all the eminent teachers, to whom can I repent?"

Un-mun answered, "Appearance."

Another student asked, "Of the three bodies—form body, consciousness body, and Dharma body—which one speaks the truth?"

Un-mun said, "Primary."

Thus Un-mun, with his short answers, opened many minds.

98. Ko Bong Explains a Poem

A student came to Zen Master Ko Bong, Seung Sahn Soensa's teacher, and said,

" 'From the ten directions all people come together.
Each one learns not-doing.
This is the field of becoming Buddha.
Empty mind passes the test and comes back.'

"Do these words help people or not?"

Ko Bong said, "They do."

"Which sentence helps them?"

"Bring each one here."

"What is the first sentence: 'From the ten directions all people come together'?"

"The dragon and the snake combine. Enlightenment and ignorance become mutual."

"Who learns not-doing?"

"Buddha and eminent teachers are swallowed; the eye links ground and sky."

"What is the field of becoming Buddha?"

"From West to East there are one hundred thousand, from North to South eight thousand."

"What is the last sentence: 'Empty mind passes the test and comes back'?"

"In action and in nonaction, the ancient way appears. The way is not dragged down into the chasm of turbulence."

"So in each sentence nature is seen. Each one is the truth."

"What have you seen and attained?"

The student shouted "KATZ!!!"

Ko Bong said, "This is taking a stick and trying to hit the moon."

99. The Story of Seung Sahn Soen-sa

Seung Sahn Soen-sa was born in 1927 in Seun Choen, North Korea. His parents were Protestant Christians.

Korea at this time was under severe Japanese military rule, and all political and cultural freedom was brutally suppressed. In 1944, Soen-sa joined the underground Korean independence movement. Within a few months he was caught by the Japanese police and narrowly escaped a death sentence. After his release from prison, he and two friends stole several thousand dollars from their parents and crossed the heavily-patrolled Manchurian border in an unsuccessful attempt to join the Free Korean Army.

In the years following World War II, while he was studying Western philosophy at Dong Guk University, the political situation in South Korea grew more and more chaotic. One day Soen-sa decided that he wouldn't be able to help people through his political activities or his academic studies. So he shaved his head and went into the mountains, vowing never to return until he had attained the absolute truth.

For three months he studied the Confucian scriptures, but he was unsatisfied by them. Then a friend of his, who was a monk in a small mountain temple, gave him the Diamond Sutra, and he first encountered Buddhism. "All things that appear in this world are transient. If you view all things that appear as never having appeared, then you will realize your true self." When he read these words, his mind became clear. For the next few weeks he read many sutras. Finally, he decided to become a Buddhist monk and was ordained in October, 1948.

Soen-sa had already understood the sutras. He realized that the only important thing now was practice. So ten days after his ordination, he went further up into the mountains and began a one-hundred-day retreat on Won Gak Mountain (the Mountain of Perfect Enlightenment). He ate only pine-needles, dried and beaten into a powder. For twenty hours every day he chanted the Great Dharani of Original Mind Energy. Several times a day he took ice-cold baths. It was a very rigorous practice.

Soon he was assailed by doubts. Why was this retreat necessary? Why did he have to go to extremes? Couldn't he go down to a small temple in a quiet valley, get married like a Japanese monk, and attain enlightenment gradually, in the midst of a happy family? One night these thoughts became so powerful that he decided to leave and packed his belongings. But the next morning his mind was clearer, and he unpacked. A few days later the same thing happened. And in the following weeks, he packed and unpacked nine times.

By now fifty days had passed, and Soen-sa's body was very exhausted. Every night he had terrifying visions. Demons would appear out of the dark and make obscene gestures at him. Ghouls would sneak up behind him and wrap their cold fingers around his neck. Enormous beetles would gnaw his legs. Tigers and dragons would stand in front of him, bellowing. He was in constant terror.

After a month of this, the visions turned into visions of delight. Sometimes Buddha would come and teach him a sutra. Sometimes Bodhisattvas would appear in gorgeous clothing and tell him that he would go to heaven. Sometimes he would keel over from exhaustion and Kwanseum Bosal would gently wake him up. By the end of eighty days, his body was strong. His flesh had turned green from the pine-needles.

One day, a week before the retreat was to finish, Soen-sa was walking outside, chanting and keeping rhythm with his *moktak*. Suddenly, two boys, eleven or twelve years old, appeared on either side of him and bowed. They were wearing many-colored robes, and their faces were of an unearthly beauty. Soen-sa was very surprised. His mind felt powerful and perfectly clear, so how could these demons have materialized? He walked ahead on the narrow mountain path, and the two boys followed him, walking right through the boulders on either side of the path. They walked together in silence for a half-hour, then, back at the altar, when Soen-sa got up from his bow, they were gone. This happened every day for a week.

Finally it was the hundredth day. Soen-sa was outside chanting and hitting the *moktak.* All at once his body disappeared, and he was in infinite space. From far away he could hear the *moktak* beating, and the sound of his own voice. He remained in this state for some time. When he returned to his body, he understood. The rocks, the river, everything he could see, everything he could hear, all this was his true self. All things are exactly as they are. The truth is just like this.

Soen-sa slept very well that night. When he woke up the next morning, he saw a man walking up the mountain, then some crows flying out of a tree. He wrote the following poem:

> The road at the bottom of Won Gak Mountain
> is not the present road.
> The man climbing with his backpack
> is not a man of the past.
> Tok, tok, tok—his footsteps
> transfix past and present.
> Crows out of a tree.
> Caw, caw, caw.

Soon after he came down from the mountain, he met Zen Master Ko Bong, whose teacher had been Zen Master Mang Gong. Ko Bong was reputed to be the most brilliant Zen Master in Korea, and one of the most severe. At this time he was teaching only laymen; monks, he said, were not ardent enough to be good Zen students. Soen-sa wanted to test his enlightenment with Ko Bong, so he went to him with a *moktak* and said, "What is this?" Ko Bong took the *moktak* and hit it. This was just what Soen-sa had expected him to do.

Soen-sa then said, "How should I practice Zen?"

Ko Bong said, "A monk once asked Zen Master Jo-ju, 'Why did Bodhidharma come to China?' Jo-ju answered, 'The pine tree in the front garden.' What does this mean?"

Soen-sa understood, but he didn't know how to answer. He said, "I don't know."

Ko Bong said, "Only keep this don't-know mind. That is true Zen practice."

That spring and summer, Soen-sa did mostly working Zen. In the fall, he sat for a hundred-day meditation session at Su Dok Sa monastery, where he learned Zen language and Dharma-combat. By the winter, he began to feel that the monks weren't practicing hard enough, so he decided to give them some help. One night, as he was on guard-duty (there had been some burglaries), he took all the pots and pans out of the kitchen and arranged them in a circle in the front yard. The next night, he turned the Buddha on the main altar toward the wall and took the incense-burner, which was a national treasure, and hung it on a persimmon tree in the garden. By the second morning the whole monastery was in an uproar. Rumours were flying around about lunatic burglars, or gods coming from the mountain to warn the monks to practice harder.

The third night, Soen-sa went to the nuns' quarters, took seventy pairs of nuns' shoes and put them in front of Zen Master Dok Sahn's room, displayed as in a shoe store. But this time, a nun woke up to go to the outhouse and, missing her shoes, she woke up everyone in the nuns' quarters. Soen-sa was caught. The next day he was brought to trial. Since most of the monks voted to give him another chance (the nuns were unanimously against him), he wasn't expelled from the monastery. But he had to offer formal apologies to all the high monks.

First he went to Dok Sahn and bowed. Dok Sahn said, "Keep up the good work."

Then he went to the head nun. She said, "You've made a great deal too much commotion in this monastery, young man." Soen-sa laughed and said, "The whole world is already full of commotion. What can you do?" She couldn't answer.

Next was Zen Master Chun Song, who was famous for his wild actions and obscene language. Soen-sa bowed to him and said, "I killed all the Buddhas of past, present, and future. What can you do?"

Chun Song said, "Aha!" and looked deeply into Soen-sa's eyes. Then he said, "What did you see?"

Soen-sa said, "You already understand."

Chun Song said, "Is that all?"

Soen-sa said, "There's a cuckoo singing in the tree outside the window."

Chun Song laughed and said, "Aha!" He asked several more questions, which Soen-sa answered without difficulty. Finally, Chun Song leaped up and danced around Soen-sa, shouting, "You are enlightened! You are enlightened!" The news spread quickly, and people began to understand the events of the preceding days.

On January 15, the session was over, and Soen-sa left to see Ko Bong. On the way to Seoul, he had interviews with Zen Master Keum Bong and Zen Master Keum Oh. Both gave him *inga,* the seal of validation of a Zen student's great awakening.

Soen-sa arrived at Ko Bong's temple dressed in his old patched retreat clothes and carrying a knapsack. He bowed to Ko Bong and said, "All the Buddhas turned out to be a bunch of corpses. How about a funeral service?"

Ko Bong said, "Prove it!"

Soen-sa reached into his knapsack and took out a dried cuttlefish and a bottle of wine. "Here are the leftovers from the funeral party."

Ko Bong said, "Then pour me some wine."

Soen-sa said, "Okay. Give me your glass."

Ko Bong held out his palm.

Soen-sa slapped it with the bottle and said, "That's not a glass, it's your hand!" Then he put the bottle on the floor.

Ko Bong laughed and said, "Not bad. You're almost done. But I have a few questions for you." He proceeded to ask Soen-sa the most difficult of the seventeen-hundred traditional Zen *kong-ans*. Soen-sa answered without hindrance.

Then Ko Bong said, "All right, one last question. The mouse eats cat-food, but the cat-bowl is broken. What does this mean?"

Soen-sa said, "The sky is blue, the grass is green."

Ko Bong shook his head and said, "No."

Soen-sa was taken aback. He had never missed a Zen question before. His face began to grow red as he gave one "like this" answer after another. Ko Bong kept shaking his head. Finally Soen-sa exploded with anger and frustration. "Three Zen Masters have given me *inga*! Why do you say I'm wrong?!"

Ko Bong said, "What does it mean? Tell me."

For the next fifty minutes, Ko Bong and Soen-sa sat facing each other, hunched like two tomcats. The silence was electric. Then, all of a sudden, Soen-sa had the answer. It was "just like this."

When Ko Bong heard it, his eyes grew moist and his face filled with joy. He embraced Soen-sa and said, "You are the flower; I am the bee."

On January 25, 1949, Soen-sa received from Ko Bong the Transmission of Dharma, thus becoming the Seventy-Eighth Patriarch in this line of succession. It was the only Transmission that Ko Bong ever gave.

After the ceremony, Ko Bong said to Soen-sa, "For the next three years you must keep silent. You are a free man. We will meet again in five hundred years."

Soen-sa was now a Zen Master. He was twenty-two years old.

100. What Is Love?

One evening, after a Dharma talk at the Cambridge Zen Center, a student asked Seung Sahn Soen-sa, "What is love?"

Soen-sa said, "I ask you: what is love?"

The student was silent.

Soen-sa said, "This is love."

The student was still silent.

Soen-sa said, "You ask me: I ask you. This is love."